The Hen House

The Beginning

Sandra Wentzel

ISBN

Paperback: 978-1-968985-49-3

Hardcover: 978-1-968985-53-0

LCCN: 2025917070

Published by

American Publishing Network
www.americanpublishingnetwork.com

Printed in the United States of America

Dedications

There are a few people to whom I could dedicate this book. First, my parents. They greatly influenced my development and taught me that life can be a great adventure. This allowed me to take the path that I had chosen, even though some of my choices were not in my best interest.

My twin sister, Susan, is the second person in my life from the beginning. We did everything together and were thick as thieves. I know I would not have turned out to be the person I am today if it was not for her. Being a twin has its perks, as I could see myself through her eyes: a picture image of the way I look when dressing, the way I walk, talk, and care for people. The way I learned things and why I could handle the disappointments along the way, all these things I could see in her, I would see in myself.

They all helped in their ways to influence the best road I would eventually take, but the only person who finally led me down the right road was my husband of over half a century, Rodney Wentzel.

He never asked me "Why do you want to do that?" or put me down when things did not go as planned. A man like Rodney only comes along once in a woman's lifetime. He has always been understanding, sensitive, and loving. I am not saying he is perfect, because who is? But we would always work out our problems and never go to bed angry with each other. Our communication was a strong and unspoken part of our relationship. Our love for each other would overcome any issues we may have had.

Seeing these differences and talking through them made a world of difference. He had always been there at my lowest point to pick me up and tell me that everything would be alright, and having his support made me a strong, independent woman. We sure had a lot of bad times, but the good times let us put the bad ones on the back burner and made them easier to forget. Weathering the storms and looking forward to the sunny days increased our love. I want to thank Rodney for his support and love. I will love you forever.

Acknowledgments

Susan Henne Noll, my twin sister, helped bring back the memories lost in the back of my mind. She has been with me throughout my life and will always be with me until Jesus takes us home.

Also, Nelson Thomas Henne, our older brother, protected us during our juvenile years and was always there when we needed him during the first fifteen years of our lives.

To my loving husband, Rodney Valentine Wentzel, who loved and was loved for over 60 years. May our remaining years be just as wonderful.

Inspiration

My inspiration to write about my early years came from reading Laura Ingalls Wilder's book "Little House on the Prairie," from her life story in the late 1800s, and the TV series "The Waltons," which took place during the 1930s to 1940s. Both wrote their stories from journals and diaries they kept based on their true-life experiences.

I am writing these short stories as I remember them and what family members have told me. All the events are true and did happen, and they are all based on my true-life experiences.

I tried to set the stage for each story the way it happened in my mind. I do not remember anything between the ages of one and three. After the first three years, all the events I write about happened between 1954 and 1965.

In the 1950s, my mind was not on keeping a journal or a diary. The fifties were an exciting time to be alive. It was the era of rock and roll: Elvis, The Beach Boys, Chubby Checker, and many other artists were making their daily appearances on TV programs like American Bandstand. I just wanted to be part of the excitement. Looking back, I wish I had kept a journal, making this book easier to write.

About the Author

I was raised on a mountain called Cedar Top in the countryside of Pennsylvania. My twin sister and I grew up as tomboys surrounded by many foster boys. Our wonderful parents were not considered poor, but they had little money.

Susie and I spent most of our time together since being the only girls among boys was not an easy adjustment. School was worse; we were bullied and treated as outcasts. We never felt as if we belonged.

Writing this book, I could finally release all the bottled-up feelings of hate and regain my self-esteem by letting go of the frustration I was holding on to for over 60 years. I am now free to live out my remaining years in complete peace and love myself once again.

I always wonder why things happen in a person's life that set the stage for how a person sees the world from birth until they die. I believe that God has a path.

Table of Contents

The Depression

Those who lived through the Depression can only remember one of the worst times in American history. Those born later can only imagine the hardships inflicted on our loved ones. Having a house over our heads and food on the table every day, along with a great job to support the family, was something we all wished for.

My mom and dad had known these hardships and managed to live and thrive while everything around them was so dismal. My dad, Wert Ruffus Henne was born on May 14, 1927, in Shartlesville, Pennsylvania, a small town outside Reading. He was six feet tall and had an average build, but what made him stand out from the other young men was the envy women had for his naturally thick, curly, blond Hair. His blonde hair was piled on his head like a crown. Women who were lucky enough to have any money would pay, what seemed to be, a huge amount to get what nature gave my dad for free. My dad was carefree and took things as they came to him. Even though he was carefree, he was very close to his parents. He did what he was told, but still had a mind of his own. His mom and dad, my grandparents (whom I never met), passed away before I was born. Dad and Grandfather worked hard to make ends meet during the Depression, but when the

Depression started to affect Grandfather's income, he began to drink to the point that eventually they lost the house and farm.

Dad said, "My father had a hard time dealing with losing everything he had worked so hard for."

The only thing with trying to forget his financial problem was that he also forgot his family. Grandfather eventually found a job working for another family on their farm. Having a job where he could support his family was not like working on his farm, so he still did a lot of drinking, and over time, it got worse.

Dad would drive the tractor to and from the fields and help bring in the crops. He said that he did not mind working on a farm that did not belong to his family.

Dad recalled that before the Great Depression, his mother and father owned land, and working on it was a pleasure knowing that one day it would belong to him and his brothers. My dad and his brothers and sisters had many chores before school. After school, there were just as many, so there was no time for schoolwork. Grandfather was of very little help and hardly left the house. Dad liked going to school, where he could dream of a better life and forget about the hard work waiting for him when he got home. He would dream of someday getting a great education and becoming a successful businessman. He knew that this was only a dream, and the day finally came when the work on the farm was more important to his family than his schooling. He had to quit school in the eighth grade and devote all his time to the farm.

With all his hardships, he told me one day that he had a "hard, but good life and would not trade it in for a different one."

Since I never met or knew my grandparents, when my dad talked about them, it was like he was talking about strangers I was supposed to have feelings for. Although Dad's parents seem like somebody I would read about in a book, I still wish I could have gotten to know them in a grandparent/ granddaughter relationship. I missed having two sets of grandparents. Dad worked hard for the little family he had, but in many respects, my mom did not have it much better.

Mom was different in many aspects, but they both had the Great Depression to deal with. My Mom; Marie Ida Bailey was born, on May 25, 1927. She was born into a much larger family. She had three sisters and five brothers. I only found out when I was an adult that there was a rumor that Grandfather Morris Bailey had many affairs. These affairs resulted in a few more children. Mom's sister told me that Grandfather would never come home after work. I cannot confirm this rumor or disprove it. I always thought that my grandparents had a happy marriage. Grandmother never said anything or gave any hint that things were anything but great between them. There was just no evidence. My mom never lived at home. Instead, she lived with one of her cousins until she was 12 years old. I never knew the cousin's real name, and we as children would only call her 'Nanna.' Her husband's name was Ed. I never found out how much Nanna influenced my mom's life. I only got bits and pieces of the story of how and why she did what she did. Whether this was due to my grandfather's affairs and his not coming home at night, I will never know. Both Nanna and Ed were nice to my sister and me. We would always go to town and spend time with them. But still, there are times when I wish that I had never found out about my grandfather's illicit affairs. There may be aunts and uncles all over the place that I have never met. Mom was only a little over five feet tall and had raven black hair; she was a natural beauty. Growing up during the Depression was so hard for her, too. Mom also had to quit school in 8th grade and go to work to help support the family.

At the start of the Depression, Mom's parents had their own business, and everyone worked to ensure that no one went hungry. During the Depression, business dropped off, so everyone had to go to work. Grandfather owned a junkyard and also worked on some cars. Aunt Helen told me that she and some of her friends would take the trunk lids off the old cars and use them as sleds in the winter. Mom never got a chance to do this since she lived in town with her cousin and not in the country, where the rest of her brothers and sisters lived.

In the mid-1930s, there were only a few county sewer systems. Grandfather also had a second business, drilling wells and installing septic tanks for those who could still afford them. Every one of Mom's brothers helped my grandfather make this a thriving business. Grandfather's business increased after World War II when the new housing boom took effect. Thousands of discharged men were coming home from the service and looking to build a new home. Grandfather and his family were lucky enough to cash in on the growth that was taking place. New homes were popping up all over, and life was great for those who could take advantage of the prosperity. On the other hand, many people never recovered from the loss they sustained due to the Great Depression of the 1930s. This is not to say that Mom and her parents had it easy. I was told again, with no evidence, and taken with a grain of salt, because of grandfather's running around at night. There was very little money. It was hard for grandmother to understand why, with a thriving business, there was no money. Mom came home to live with her parents right after her 12th birthday, and by this time, she had gained a lot of weight. The doctors told my grandmother that she had a slow metabolism. She was a chunky 12-year-old.

Over the next few years, she managed to slim down and became a beautiful teenager. It was only a few years after this that she met my dad. Mom always seemed to have more love inside her than she knew what to do with. She would always bring home stray animals and want to keep them. She would call them her babies and take great care of them.

Grandmother said, "She would always cry when it was time to set them free."

This love she had for life would stay with her throughout the rest of her life. My mom was just like any other girl growing up during the Depression. Her clothes were handmade out of whatever fabric could be found at the time. She, like my dad, had lots of chores to do before and after school. I cannot imagine what life for her was like.

Mom and Dad

The Forever Love

I believe she would not have become such a strong woman if it were not for the era she grew up in. If it was not bad enough that Mom and Dad had to live during the Depression, World War II came shortly after. Mom and Dad were no exception to the hardships of war. Many people were starting to get their lives back together after the depression ended when the unthinkable happened; the Japanese bombed Pearl Harbor on December 7, 1941. Many men were ready to give up their lives to defend their country. The government had just enacted the draft, and at this time, Dad was too young to be drafted.

He knew one day his time would come when he was old enough. Since no one knew how long this war would last, Dad knew that one year, the letter would come from the war department. He was still working hard on the farm, trying to make a living. Mom, meanwhile, was working in a laundry somewhere in Reading, I never found out the extra location. As the war raged on, there were many injured and dying men and women. The hospitals were full, and there were many sheets to be washed.

Mom said, "I did not mind working in a laundry because I was doing my part to support those brave men and women fighting on the front lines."

Working in the laundry had one drawback: it got so hot with all of the washing machines and dryers running, she could not keep a wave in her beautiful black hair. One of mom's best friends at the laundry just happened to be dad's sister and she was the one who introduced them to each other. Dad would drive his sister to and from work every day.

Every evening Dad would arrive a few minutes early and stand at the rail about ten feet from where his sister and my mom were working. Watching from the rail, one day he noticed the most beautiful, dark-haired girl he had ever seen. She was folding sheets to be shipped to the hospitals in the Reading area. On the way home that day, he asked his sister who she was. His sister told him all about my mom and the little she knew about her family.

She also stated, "She would introduce him to her if he liked."

Well, he did not hesitate with an answer and only wanted to know when. This was just his luck that the work week had ended, and he would have to wait a full weekend to meet her. Needless to say, that was a very long weekend for Dad.

He asked his sister several times, "Do you think she will like me?"

"Of course she will," was her reply. Dad was so intrigued by her that he forgot to ask his sister her name.

Monday finally came, and on the way to the laundry, Dad asked his sister her name. "Marie Bailey," she said.

Dad was a very sensitive and shy man. He was not sure if he could go through with the introduction to such a pretty girl as Marie. He saw himself as only a poor country boy with very little education. He was sure that Marie would turn him down, but he wanted badly to ask her on a date.

His sister told him, "Not to worry," that she had become good friends and knew she would at least give him a chance. Dad, being so shy, reluctantly said "Ok."

Since there was no work on the weekend, by Monday, there were a lot of sheets to be washed and dried. Since there was so much work to be done, Dad would have to wait until he could return in the evening to make himself known to Marie. The evening finally came, and the sun was going down around 4:00 p.m., dad still had a few more rows in the field to plow. Each row seemed to be getting longer than the last. Even though he had only been plowing for approximately four hours, he said, "It seems more like days have gone by."

As he ended his plowing, he could see some dark clouds

starting to roll over the mountain. The fields were pretty dry and could use some rain. Dad knew it would be raining soon, and he still had to drive to Reading. Since he spent so much time in the field, he had very little time to eat the supper his mom had made for him. He only had a few minutes to eat, wash up, and change his clothes before leaving to pick up his sister. As he opened the front door to leave, the wind had picked up, and the dust and leaves were swirling around. The thunder and lightning had begun, and the rain was pouring down. As he was recalling this stressful time in his life, he told me he thought he was going to have a heart attack.

He wanted to get to the laundry in plenty of time; missing Mom would mean another day of waiting. Boy! I am so glad he made it through that day, or I may not be here to write about it. He started the old car, the only one his family could afford, and went to meet his fate. It was roughly a half-hour drive to the laundry. Dad again stood at the railing where he had stood so many times before. This rail separated the walkway from the working area. He could feel sweat beading up on his forehead, and it began to roll down his face. He did not know if it was because he was so nervous to meet Mom or just because of the heat in the room. He kept watching the clock on the wall. The storm raging outside was getting worse, and he could hear the rain pounding on the ceiling of the building, along with his heart thumping in his chest.

The thunder was cracking, and the lightning strikes would light up the dimly lit room where Mom was working. It was finally 5:00, and the stop-work bell rang. His sister clocked out before Mom and saw Dad waiting. She did not say anything to him. Knowing the tension Dad was under, she did not want to make matters worse for him. In the distance, he saw Mom walking toward the time clock and placing her time card in. He knew his sister would soon be introducing them. As his sister and Mom gathered up their belongings and walked toward Dad, he said he felt like he was going to faint. This was love at first sight, but he still did not know if Mom would feel the same. Dad met his sister and Marie on the walkway.

His sister then said, "Wert, this is Marie."

Dad could not find his tongue, but he did manage to say "Pleased to meet you." Dad hardly caught his breath, then said, "Would you like a ride home?"

Her reply stunned him when she said, "No, I already have a ride, my brother is picking me up soon." Dad knew for sure that he had blown it, Marie did not like him. Then he could not believe his ears when she said, "But I would like to see you again sometime."

She gave him her phone number and said "Please call me."

Dad and his sister waited with her until her brother came to pick her up. Marie's brother seemed to be very nice and said that he was glad to meet Dad. Dad was on cloud nine by this time. He could not stop talking about her all the way home. Dad said that he was so glad to be home knowing that Marie wanted to see him again.

Later that evening, Dad dialed Marie's phone number with the phone shaking in his hand. As the phone started to ring, Dad could feel his mouth getting dry. To his surprise, it was not Marie on the other end but her mother.

After she said "Hello," Dad asked if he could talk to Marie.

Her mother said, "Oh yes, you must be the nice man Marie has talked about. Here Marie is now," she replied.

As Marie picked up the phone, Dad heard Marie and her mother talking in the background. He was never sure what they were saying, but he knew by the tone of their voices, Marie was glad he called.

Marie picked up the phone and said "Hi," Just hearing her voice made him feel more at ease. Dad said they talked for about half an hour. She did agree to go out with him on a date the following Saturday.

Again, the wait and the sight of her every day when he would go to the laundry to pick up his sister at work seemed like months, not just days. While Dad stood at the rail every day watching Marie, she would give him a big smile. He knew by this time that he was feeling excitement more than fear. Saturday, Dad picked up Marie at 7 p.m. and took her to dinner. He was unsure how long the date would go on, but to his amazement, everything went very well. From then on, they saw each other as often as they could. Within six months of meeting Marie, she and Dad were engaged to be married.

They agreed that the date for their wedding would be January 8th, 1946. As the day approached, Dad again had the sweats and was very nervous. Getting married at the end of World War II was not the best timing. It was a small wedding with only a few people attending. Now that mom and dad were married, the first thing was to find a house they could call home, seal their love, and start a family. They found a small house to rent in Blandon, Pennsylvania, a few miles north of Reading.

Life During World War II

As if it were not bad enough that Mom and Dad had to live through the Depression, World War II came quickly after. The fighting was mainly across the sea in Europe, so Mom and Dad were not too worried at this time, but then just like that, the world and their lives were turned upside down. The Japanese Attacked Pearl Harbor on December 7th, 1941. Many people had just started to get their lives back together when the war started. Mom and Dad were no exception. At this time, Dad was of drafting age and did not want to leave Mom, but there were thousands of young men who did not want to enter a war where they knew they might die.

With the United States entering the war, the national draft was enacted. When Dad turned 18 in 1945, he had to register for the draft. As their love grew, they thought there was nothing that would separate them. They had just lived in their new home for a few weeks when all their dreams came crashing down. Their world was about to fall apart. The dreadful letter they knew was coming one day was finally placed in their mailbox. Mom knew as soon as she took the mail out of the box and saw the address that their lives were going to change significantly. Dad was still working on the railroad and did not know about the letter until later that night.

When Dad arrived home, Mom was crying, he knew what her tears were saying. Dad being drafted was no surprise, but it still upset both of them. He was drafted on March 6, 1946. Since their wedding, they prayed that this day would never come. The war had ended in Europe, Hitler was dead, and the Japanese in the Pacific had surrendered, but the cleanup in Germany and many other countries was still underway. Dad would be part of this process.

Dad knew he would be in the army for at least 2 years. As the time came closer for him to leave, they both felt their happiness being washed away. Dad was getting ready to go and leave his new bride behind. The day finally came for Dad to leave, and his heart was breaking, and waves of tears overwhelmed him. They knew that basic training would take at least 6 weeks. Knowing this felt like forever, but all they could do was hope for the best. Dad kept a positive outlook, telling Mom that at least the war was over and he would not be in combat.

Mom wanted to hold on to him forever when the bus was seen making the turn onto their street. Dad gave Mom one more hug and a big kiss and then stepped onto the bus. As the door closed behind him, he rushed to a window seat to see Mom as the bus pulled away.

She whispered to herself, "Is this happening?" She slowly walked back to the house to continue crying.

She said that she did not know when the tears would stop flowing.

Dad said, "It seemed forever to get to Fort Knox, Kentucky," where his basic training would begin.

A few days later, after he had arrived at boot camp, he got a letter stating that his wife was pregnant. He was unsure how to feel, knowing he likely would be shipped overseas. He was correct, his orders came through, and he was going to Germany in a few days. He was so down that he just wanted to see mom again.

He said that everyone got a three-day pass before leaving for Germany. He made a scary decision; he decided he would try to get back to Pennsylvania to see Mom and hope he would make it back in time without being marked AWOL. Going so far away was not a wise decision, but he needed to see Mom at least one more time. He said that he did not know how he managed to get to Pennsylvania, but he did it. Mom was surprised to see him but told him he needed to leave to go back to camp. He was thrilled to see her, but also concerned about leaving his pregnant wife behind but he knew he had no choice and only spent a few hours before rushing back to Kentucky. He made it back in the nick of time. The other soldiers were getting their things together. Since Dad was gone longer than most soldiers, he did not receive the items needed for the trip. Dad was off to Germany, and Mom had to work harder to pay the rent.

After all, there was a new baby on its way. No one knew if Dad would have to serve the full 2 years. Dad said that the flight to Germany seemed to take forever, approximately 12 hours.

Arriving in Germany during the first week of March 1946. He said, "It was a thrill for him since he had never been any farther than the nearby county north of Reading in all of his life."

The surroundings were strange but unique. He could not understand the language but found the German People very friendly. As thrilling as all this was, he still could not get his mind off his lovely pregnant wife so far away. He had been working hard while in Germany, but could not wait to go home. He was learning to drive a large Military Tank, but hoping he would never have to drive it in wartime. He was just about to go into training to be a paratrooper when his new orders came through. To this day, I can't believe that he would have jumped out of an airplane, but then who knows?

Since Mom was expecting and the war was over, Dad lucked out and was sent home only after ten months of service. He was not discharged in time to make it home for the birth of their first child, a beautiful baby boy who they named Nelson Henne. Dad was still in Germany for a few more months.

Dad said that what he experienced in Germany would stay with him for the rest of his life. He saw things that would change the way he felt about humanity.

Seeing the hardship, the destruction, and the pain on the people's faces had a profound impact on the way he viewed life. Seeing how many lives were destroyed and watching those people trying to pick up what was left of their lives and go on. He saw the cruelness that a war of this magnitude could cause. There were still people dying every day from sickness, starvation, and just being out in the elements during harsh weather. Many no longer had a home to go back to, so living on the streets was the norm. Dad said that, at times, he felt so helpless that he could only do so much. Supplies were slow to arrive, but when they did come, he could not wait to get them distributed.

Living on a small farm, he never had much, but at times he felt rich compared to the refugees in Germany. The only thing that gave him any peace was knowing that the residents of Germany were no longer in danger from a madman. Seeing the people sharing the little they had and pulling everything together to rebuild was enlightening and brought hope. As the day and hours passed by, dad would sit at night and write letters home to mom. Letting her know he was safe and trying to describe what he saw and how he spent his days. Since dad only had an 8th-grade education, writing letters was difficult. He knew what he wanted to say, but putting the words down on paper was difficult. There were nights when he was not at the barracks and had to sleep under the stars. As he would lay, looking up at the night sky would take him back to the farm in Pennsylvania. Watching the storm clouds slowly moving across the sky and feeling the rain starting to fall, took him back to the first day he met Mom. He was glad he never had to go into combat, but seeing the devastation was unforgettable.

Over time, he made peace with what he saw and prayed to God to help him give whatever he could and help the people get on with their lives. Seeing the Children receiving food and kindness from his fellow soldiers made his days bearable. The weather and landscape were much like Pennsylvania. There were mountains and flat lands. There were streams and rivers. The winter seems colder than those in Pennsylvania, but the summers were not as hot. The changing of the season helped give some normality to the passing days. Dad said he would count each day, for when he would be on that long flight home. Being a dad, and having a son, who was now over 5 months old, gave him the feeling that he was missing so much of the early years of his son's life. To his surprise, his orders came through one day stating that he was being discharged and was going home. He was so happy that the tears overwhelmed him. His dream had come true, and the nightmare of being away from his wife and son was over.

The Homecoming

Dad was finally home, and Mom could not have been more thrilled. She said that he "seemed to have lost some weight and his blonde curly hair was much shorter, but she did not care."

All she wanted was for him to be safe and in her arms again. His son was as cute as ever, and Dad was so proud. They lived in the tiny little house for a few more years. Dad knew he had to get a better-paying job to support his wife and child. He looked around for a few months and landed a job with a company known as the "Parish." It was a factory that made truck body frames. Dad was hired as a welder. He had no experience as a welder but was a fast learner. He was making a good wage, and the work was pretty steady. More than anything, he wanted to own a home of his own.

It took a few months, but Mom and Dad had enough money to buy a small piece of land on top of a mountain in a newly developing community called "Cedar Top." Even though Dad only had minimum education, he was still qualified and had the skills to build a home.

In 1948, regulations and permits were not much of an issue when building a home. Dad had plenty of help with the construction. Mom's brothers helped as well, but Dad did most of the work himself. Partway through the construction Mom told Dad that she was going to have a baby again.

At that point, Dad had an urgency to get the house built and finished. The size of the house was going to be three small bedrooms, a living room, a kitchen, and one Bath.

Thank God that Dad was a strong young man. He would go to "Cedar Top" every evening after work to continue to work on the house. Mom said it was like having him away in the army again because she hardly ever saw him. He would come home after dark only to eat, kiss her and Nelson goodnight, and then go to bed. He was so tired every night that my mom was worried he would get sick.

Two New Chicks

It was the beginning of a new year in 1949, and Dad was close to finishing the house. Mom's due date was getting close, so Dad could not work on the house as much as he would have liked.

On January 27, 1949, two beautiful baby girls made their entrance into the world. I was named Sandra Marlene Henne, and my twin sister was named Susan Marie Henne.

Having twins was a surprise to both Mom and Dad. Now they had three small children to feed. Dad was working extra hard, and now, here we were.

Mom said she could "see the stress in his eyes." Mom and Dad took us home to the small house that they were renting. They were so glad to know the new house would soon be ready. The rented house was so cold and drafty that Mom would take one of us and Dad would take the other and lay us on their chest overnight, to keep us warm. We only had to live in the rented house for a few more months till the new house was finally ready. To parents of this decade, one child was more than enough to raise, but having three would take a lot of work. But being so young, they had both the energy and love to take on the task.

The Bond

Since the day of my birth on that cold day in January, I have never looked back on what my life could have been. I guess the reason was that I knew I would never be alone. I was born first by only fifteen minutes. There are those people who hate their names, but not me. I always thought of my name as being that of a strong, beautiful person.

Growing up I was plain and unassuming, but I never saw myself as being ugly.

Susan says, to this day, "We may have never been born if she had not pushed me out."

But then I tell her, "I was ready to be born and was just waiting for her to grow a little bit more."

There are times that I think I waited too long, only because at our birth, she was a little bit bigger than I was. But even with the slight weight difference, it was hard for people who did not know us, to tell us apart. The only way Mom and Dad could tell us apart was that I was born with a birthmark on the outside of my left wrist. The story behind the birthmark is that when Mom and Dad were first married, Dad raised raccoons.

One day, Mom went outside through the screen door, when a large raccoon jumped down from the roof, and she put her arm up to protect her face. He hit her on her left wrist. She only had a small scratch from the raccoon's tiny paw. A raccoon's nails are very sharp, but in a few days, the scratch was gone and they never thought anything else about it until I was born.

As mom examined my body to be sure I had all my fingers and toes, she noticed the red mark on my wrist. As mom looked closer, it seemed to be a small animal paw with a pad and four to five tiny toes. It's located at a perfect place so only a few close family and friends know it is there. I would always tell the story of Mom and the raccoon when asked about my birthmark. I am unsure if I believe the story or not, but it gives a good explanation for a puzzling mark.

Susie and I looked alike until we were adults when aging gave us a slightly different look. We still look enough alike that we are still mistaken for each other. Now we are married and living on our own. We were never far apart from each other as the years went by. We would always protect and defend each other; we created our own personalities without losing the bond most twins share. I believe that God played a huge role in the direction in which my life has gone. The love of both family and friends early in my life helped me prepare for the difficulties I faced in the future, so I could have an extraordinary life.

Being a twin has its advantages. We could share clothes, do everything together, and always have a friend close by, so you were never alone. And no need for a mirror, always knowing what you look like.

On the other hand, there are some disadvantages too. Like having very little privacy, feeling the pain of the other, and having others see you as one of two and never as you as a person. Since it would take many years for our personalities to emerge.

In a way, I loved having my sister close. We could do things that most children could not do. There was one time when we were only three years old when I thought I was losing a part of myself.

Being born a twin came along with some health problems. Our eyesight was never that great. At an early age, Mom and Dad could see that something was not quite right with our eyes. They could see that our eyes would cross. This meant that both of our eyes were not working together; while one was looking one way, the other eye was looking another way.

At this young age, we both had to wear eyeglasses. Susie's eyes were worse than mine. By the age of four, my eyes seemed stable, and wearing eyeglasses corrected the defect. While I was improving, Susie's eyes were getting worse.

Mom and Dad were told that I would always need eyeglasses. I did not understand what was happening or why Susie would go with Mom to see the eye doctor, but I did not need to go. Susie seemed to be drifting away from me, and I felt I would never see her again.

Being only four years old, I still remember it like it was yesterday. All I knew was that one day, Mom left early in the morning with Susie. A few hours later, she came home without her. I was so upset and confused. I remember crying and had to be calmed down.

Mom told me what had happened and that "Susie had to have an operation on her one eye and would be gone for a few days."

Again, I had no idea what she was trying to tell me, what an operation was, or where she was. Back in the 50s, there was nothing like day surgery. Coming home the same day was not known at this time.

The next few days went by so slowly, each day I would ask, "Where is Susie?"

The day had arrived for her to come home. Still not knowing where she was or what had happened to her, Mom assured me that I would be with my sister later on that day. Even though small children were not allowed on the patient floors. Mom waited for

Dad to come home, and we all went to the hospital to pick up Susie.

We arrived at the hospital in about twenty minutes, and we all went inside. In the Lobby Dad and I waited for Mom to come down the elevator.

"Why is it taking so long?" I asked my dad.

I still could not comprehend where we were and why Susie had to stay there, but all I knew was that I was going to have my sister back again. The elevator door opened, and Mom was holding Susie in her arms. I ran over to her, and Mom put her down. We hugged for a few minutes before walking with Mom back over to Dad. Mom took Susie's hand while Dad took my hand, and we all walked out of the hospital door together.

Susie had a patch on her one eye for a few days. After the third day, Mom had to switch the eye patch back and forth for over a week. Later in life, when I could understand what had happened, I was told that this was to ensure that both eyes could get their strength back at the same time. If the patch stayed on one eye all the time, the muscle in the eye with the patch would get weaker while the eye without the patch would get stronger. Susie's last visit to the eye doctor had come and gone, and Susie's eyes were now stable. We both would need glasses for the rest of our lives. Again, we were twins. After this experience, we were never far apart.

I find it amazing that two people can experience the same events, but years later we recall them differently or not at all. There are many events in our lives that Susie remembers that I do not and the same for her. We lived the same life and did the same things most of the time. I have talked to her about her experience with her eyes, and she does not remember it as clearly as I do.

In a way, her memories of some of the events in our lives that I did not remember, helped me fill in some of the gaps. We were now five years old and starting school in a few months.

Growing Up

While Susie and I were getting ready to start school, Mom had put on some weight. She was now close to three hundred pounds. Dad never seemed to mind her weight gain, he would always see her as his beautiful Marie. Despite her weight mom was still very active. Having a house full of kids kept her busy, so she did not have time to relax.

Starting school was a turning point in my life. Mom would take us shopping for new clothes. In the 1950s, all girls were required to wear a dress to school. I slightly remember a plaid dress or two. I do not remember how we got to and from school, but I am sure it had to be a bus.

The first Elementary school we went to was built in the late 1800s and was located in Kenhorst, a community right outside of Reading. It was still operational in the 1940s. The Fairview Elementary School burned down in 1949.

It was rebuilt, and the existing students were sent to surrounding schools. There was no central school district at this time. In 1944, the new Governor Mifflin School District was formed. Fairview was now a part of this district.

In September 1954, Susie and I attended Kindergarten at the Fairview Elementary School for a short time. The only thing I remember about Fairview is a large sliding board inside one of the oversized rooms. If my memory serves me right, there was also a sandbox in the same room. We were then transferred to the Yocum School for the first and second grades.

The third grade was a unique time in our lives. We were now attending the third grade at Cedar Top Elementary School. This school was only down the road, approximately one-quarter mile from where we lived, and had two classrooms. We could walk to and from school in approximately fifteen minutes. It was only a two-story red brick building. The third grade was on the first floor and the fourth grade was on the second floor. There was only one set of bathrooms and a single coat room on the first floor. There was no lunchroom, all lunches had to be brought from home. There was a small playground with a few swings and sliding boards. I remember that school fondly.

We were again only there a few months when the new Governor Mifflin Elementary, Junior High, and Senior High Schools were ready for students to attend. The following year was 1957, and we started the school year at the new elementary school in Shillington. We had a wonderful older lady as our third-grade teacher. Her name was Mrs. Mathias. Out of all the teachers in my life, she was the best. She had lots of patience and understanding for all of her young students.

Susie and I on the First day of School

Susie and I were in the same class up to the 6th Grade. After that, I do not know whose idea it was to separate us and place us in different classes with a different teacher. We had come to depend on each other for homework and support in studying for a test, but now we were on our own. In a way, I guess it was for the best. It gave us a chance to think for ourselves, but it took some getting used to. We never had the same homework or learned the same things, at the same time, for the rest of our school years.

When we arrived at the Shillington Elementary School, Susie would hop on another bus that would take her up to the Yocum school building. She would spend her full day there. Around 3 in the afternoon, she would return to the Shillington building to join me on the bus ride home. The trip home took around 30 minutes. Susie and I would discuss how our day went. We would compare homework assignments to see if we could help each other later that night. Even though we had different homework, we could still share what needed to be done with each other.

Grade six was a trying year for me. Since Susie was at another school with another teacher, she did not experience having the Principal as a Teacher. His name was Mr. Charingo. He was an overbearing and strict teacher, holding on to a ruler all the time whenever he was teaching. He was a large and imposing man, standing over six feet tall with a bald head. A few of the boys in my class did not take well to an overpowering man ordering them around. I always wondered how a student with a large attitude and ego made it to the sixth grade.

One boy did not do his homework and had not been doing it for weeks. Mr. Charingo, being very strict decided it was time for this boy to be punished. Hitting or striking a student was still accepted in schools at this time. The teacher told the student to rise and walk up to his desk. All that time when the boy was walking up through the rows of desks, he would look back and laugh. He was defiant and refused to let the teacher make an example of him.

The boy stood in front of the teacher's desk with a look of contempt on his face. Mr. Charingo approached the boy, who was also very large for his age, and told him, "Put out your hands, palms up."

The boy stood there as if he did not hear the teacher's request. As Mr. Charingo reached out to grab one of the boys' hands. The boy grabbed the teacher's hand and pushed him to the floor. The teacher hit his head, and there was some blood trickling down the side of his face. Seeing such violence right before my eyes, I gasped and could not believe what had happened.

Mr. Charingo pushed himself up from the floor and told the

boy, "Get out of my classroom."

They both headed for the school office, where the boy was thrown out of school. I do not know if any other actions were taken against the boy or his parents.

I never had any problems with Mr. Charingo, but I did not like his idea of homework. We had lessons to do out of a few of our books, like reading chapters or writing about what we just read. We had a math book that would start with the basics, and halfway through the book, the problems got much harder. Our homework assignment was to do a page every night until we finished the book.

Each day, the teacher would check your work, and if you had at least one problem wrong, you had to do the same assignment all over again, until you got them all correct. Some students would finish the book in a few months by doing more than one page a night. By the end of the school year, I would have only finished half of the book. I never said I was smart.

This was when I wished Susie and I still were in the same class, helping each other every night would have made a difference in my understanding of math.

Winter Months

There were a lot of things happening at home during this time. Looking back at the age of nine, I experienced several events that have stuck with me to this day.

The winter and Christmas of 1958 were great but was also a stressful time. In late March of 1958, there was a violent snowstorm. It was a day-long blizzard that dumped 60 Inches of snow on much of Pennsylvania. Living out in the country, we were snowed in for days. Mom had prepared for the snow, and we were assured there was a lot of food in the house. I remember kneeling on the sofa and watching the snow fall through the large picture window. The Snowflakes were so large that it only took a few minutes for the snow to pile up.

I stayed on the sofa for a while, just watching Dad's car, which was parked in the driveway right in front of the house, slowly disappearing. It was late and time for bed. By morning, when I looked out of the window, I could only see the antenna of Dad's car.

We were glad we did not have to go to school, but the snow was too deep, so playing in it was out of the question. What was the point of being home from school? Mom tried to open the front door, but the snow was so high that she could barely see the sky.

Living in the country, Dad said, "It would be a long time until the plows would get us out. We just have to sit and be patient."

The next thing that happened was that the electricity went out, so the home heating system no longer worked. Dad had a small kerosene heater full of fuel in the basement. I remember him bringing it up and placing it in the kitchen. Since the house was only one floor, it was enough to keep us all warm. We all had to wear a jacket, but at least we would not freeze to death.

Dad said, "I only have enough fuel for a few days, so I hope the snow will end soon and the electricity will come back on."

We had an electric stove in the kitchen, so making any meals on it was out of the question. Mom took some Lebanon bologna out of the refrigerator and placed a few slices in a frying pan. She then placed the pan on the small space heater. As it started to fry, she poured a small amount of milk and flour mixture over the bologna. Instead of dried beef, she made the same thing with bologna. She then placed a slice of bread on a plate and poured the mixture over it. I was not so thrilled about eating this concoction, but you know what they say: *When you are hungry, you will eat anything.*

It took me a while to eat it, but it all went down to satisfy my hunger. We were snowed in for a few more days, but the electricity finally came on. We at least had a stove, a TV and heat.

As much as I was glad that we did not have to go to school, it got to the point where I was looking forward to going back. I do not know how people in the old days made it during winter with no TV. It took a few days for the plows to come up to our driveway. Mom and Dad were so glad to get the driveway cleared. Dad had been out of work for three days.

Mom knew that Dad's next paycheck would be smaller than usual, so she was careful to stay on a budget. Mom was running out of food, like milk and bread. Dad said that the roads were too bad for Mom to drive so he went to the store for her.

Listening to the radio, an announcement aired that the schools would reopen on Monday. The snow was still pretty deep, but Mom left us out to play. We could not sleigh ride, but we could at least get out of the house for a while. It took a few weeks for the snow to fade away enough for us to use our sleds. Life was finally getting back to normal.

Nelson, being a few years older than us, also wanted to get out of the house for a while. Since the snow was so deep, he decided to build an igloo. He did not have to cut blocks or anything like that. All he had to do was dig a hole in a snow pile. As he dug, he would smooth out the inside walls. It took him a few hours, and soon he had a large compartment carved out of the snow bank. He left the smaller kids to take turns going in it and sit for a few minutes. Mom was not so sure about the whole thing; she was so afraid it would cave in and bury the kids. She did not say anything for a day or so, but as the weather started to warm up a little and the snow started to melt; she no longer allowed any of the kids to go into the igloo.

The igloo was around 3 days old when Nelson noticed he could not find his glasses. By this time, the igloo had collapsed, and it was just a pile of snow. Nelson could not remember where he had put his glasses last. We all searched the house, and still, there was no sign of them.

Nelson and his igloo in winter months

A few weeks later, the snow had melted and some of the grass and ground were starting to show. Nelson could not see enough to do his schoolwork without his glasses, but he managed for a few weeks. Mom and Dad did not like waiting so long to get him a new pair, but they prayed they would be found.

One day, still looking for Nelson's glasses, Mom, by chance, was outside when she noticed a pair of glasses lying on the ground, right where the igloo had sat. She thanked God for helping her find them. She picked them up and saw that they were no worse to wear. Mom and Dad were so happy to have found them, knowing they were only a few months old. Buying new glasses was a large expense, just as they are now.

The Doll & Orange Tractors

Mom and Dad would always put up a real tree in the living room and decorate it to the hilt. Nelson, the Christmas before, had just received an American Flyer train with all the track. Dad would place his train under the tree, and we all would get a turn running it.

Mom and Dad loved Christmas as much as they loved every other holiday. They would go all out with presents. We never got just one or two, but five or six presents. Of Course, one or two of the presents were something to wear.

The Christmas of 1955 was a special Christmas for me. Susie and I unwrapped a rubber doll that would wet herself. I still remember putting on her diaper and filling the small plastic baby bottle with water. She came with three diapers, so it did not take long for each one to get wet. I would hang up the diapers until they dried. I loved that doll; as soon as the diapers would dry, I would feed her again.

Surprisingly, what I remember the most was the smell of the

rubber. To this day, if I smell an item and it has this same rubber smell, it takes me back to that wonderful Christmas day.

Remembering 1956 was another Christmas that Susie and I both remember clearly. We knew that Santa would bring us something special under the tree. As the daylight came through our bedroom windows, we knew it was time to see what Santa had brought us. They were sitting in the middle of the living room, we both, still in our pajamas, could not believe our eyes. There sat two, not one, but two large all-metal orange pedal tractors. What a unique toy. We both ran up to them and Susie got on one and I got on the other. The house that Dad built had a long hallway that stretched from the kitchen to the living room, which made a perfect place to ride our new shiny orange metal tractors.

As the years went by, there would be many more Christmases to hold in our hearts forever. Mom and Dad could always make any holiday special. They seemed to be able to come up with something new every month. Growing into a teenager, I could see all the work that mom and dad would put into the preparation for each holiday.

Enlarging The House

As much as Mom loved her family, we could all see she was getting restless. Dad would go to work every day, and Susie, Nelson, and I headed off to school, while Mom was left alone at home. Sure, you would think that taking care of all of us would be enough during the day to keep her busy, but to her, it was not

My brother Nelson with Susan and me

satisfying, and she wanted more to do.

Coming from a large family, she missed all the commotion that would go on all day. Mom and Dad had a private discussion and decided they would take in a foster child. A small child would give mom more to do and give her back that feeling of being needed during the day.

This decision came with some problems. The main one was that the house was not large enough for another child. The house, as it is, only had three bedrooms, so this meant there would have to be an addition added on. They knew this would be a great expense, so they agreed to go on with the addition.

Dad decided that the addition would be on the top of the house, making a second floor. It would be above the kitchen and a small part of the living room. The new stairway would be placed along the living room wall outside of Nelson's Bedroom. The addition would consist of four more bedrooms. Dad started work in the spring of 1957. Dad had help from Mom's brother Tom. They both worked endlessly for the rest of the spring and summer. I was unsure why they needed four more bedrooms, but this would become apparent over the next few years.

Once the second floor was done, Susie and I got to move our bedroom upstairs to one of the new rooms. Nelson also got one of the new rooms as well, which was across the hall from ours. Everything was set, and now Mom could call about a foster child.

She had been in touch with a social worker at least once a week, informing her that the addition would be finished shortly. The social worker had a small boy named Sammy, ready for Mom and Dad to take into their home. He was only around two years old and had a learning disability. Mom found this the challenge she was looking for. Mom knew that Sammy would need lots of love and understanding, and he would give her companionship during the day, which she was craving. What was a great idea in having mom feel good about herself would only grow into filling all of the spare rooms.

Within the next few months, the social worker would call Mom and ask her if she would take in another child. In approximately one & a half years, Mom and Dad had a full house of 5 new mouths to feed. They were all boys of different ages. I was never sure if this was what Dad had in mind when adding the addition.

He was never opposed to having all the boys and seemed to enjoy the company when he came home every day. A few boys lived with us for years, while others left and were returned to their families in a few months. All would depend on the situation and how fast the family could be rehabilitated. Some of the boys came from broken homes where neither their mother nor their father had the resources to provide for them, while a few of the boys were abused and needed to be removed for their safety.

Being only two girls, living in a house full of boys was not always easy. There were some perks and also some disadvantages to living with so many boys who were not your biological brothers, but somehow, we seemed to make it work.

I was never afraid, upset, or hated any of the boys. Mom had her rules, and the boys understood their roles in the household. The older boys would help with the laundry, the cleaning, and taking care of the younger boys when bathing and getting dressed. Mom made sure they had all the items needed to make living with us a pleasure and not a chore. Since mom and dad only had a seventh-grade education, they had a limit to how much they could help any of the boys with their homework. Without saying, some of the older boys would pitch in.

Seeing Social Work Up Close

I had an experience when I was only 9 years old. The Social Worker came to our home to talk to Mom, asking her if she had room for one more boy. This was a small baby.

Mom said, "What, one more?"

There was a catch to this request. There was a reason why the Social Worker came to our house without the baby. She needed someone to assist her in fetching the little boy. She asked my mom if she could take me with her. I was unsure what was involved and what was going to happen, but when she asked me if I would go with her, I agreed. I walked out and got in the Social Worker's car, and we left for town.

On the way, the social worker tried to explain to me what was going to happen. The longer she talked, the more, in the back of my mind, I would wonder if it was a good idea.

We were in the middle of the city and parked along a curb, on a one-way street. The houses were right next to each other, and they all looked the same to me.

The Social Worker opened the car door and said, "Follow, but stay back a small distance."

I watched her ring the doorbell and enter the building. I kept my distance, but close enough to see her. I watched as she walked up a flight of stairs to the second floor, keeping my distance. I had a thousand things running through my mind, and none of them were as terrifying as what I was about to witness. At the top of the steps was another door that was the entrance to a small apartment. She knocked on the door, and a young lady opened it. I could see she had been crying and did not want to let the social worker in.

They stood there and talked for what seemed like hours, but it had only been about twenty minutes when the lady finally left her in. I was not sure if I should also go in or not. I just stood on the stairs and waited for an invitation. Again, I heard a voice coming from around the corner, which I believe was the kitchen. The voices seemed to be getting louder and louder. The young lady's voice was quivering, and she started to cry hysterically.

I heard the Social Worker's voice getting louder as she told the lady, "I need to take the Baby."

The little boy was lying in a playpen right inside the door. I could see the baby clearly, and he did not look well at all, and was wet and dirty. The Social Worker stood in the doorway and said, "Come in and take the baby out of the playpen."

She told me, "Wrap him in a blanket and go out to the car."

I entered the room and grabbed a dingy gray blanket hanging on one side of the playpen. As I wrapped the baby, the young lady came to me and tried to take the baby back from my arms. By this time, she was not only crying but screaming at me to give her the baby.

The Social Worker told me to leave right away and take the baby to the car. I was shaking so badly that I was afraid I was going to drop him. I could see the social worker holding the lady back from coming down the steps. I hurried down the steps to the car, but I still could hear the lady crying and screaming at the social worker from the second-floor apartment door.

The social worker made it back to the car with the young mother right on her heels. As soon as she got in the car, she pressed the lock button on the door, as the lady was pounding on the windows. I was so scared and could not wait to get away from there. The baby was also crying and needed to be changed. We left the curb and started going home.

I asked the Social Worker, "Does this happen often?"

She said, "More times than you think."

On that day, I grew up a few more years. I learned how hard it is to do the right thing, even though it will hurt someone else. I was told that the young mother had no money and was unable to take care of the baby. When the mother shows she can care for her son, he will be returned to her. I told Mom all that had happened and that I did not want to do that ever again.

Mom told me, "Life is hard in some cases, and this is just a small part of it."

Two Small Boys

Mom knew that taking in more than one foster child would be a lot of work, as she already had one two-year-old with a learning disability. But early in the summer of 1957, she got her second chance to show how she could handle an unusual situation.

Two small boys were on their way to our house. Mom was told by the social worker that they would need a lot of patience and understanding. Mom and Dad did not care if the children who came to live with us were black, white, or purple, as long as they needed a loving family.

Susie and I had just gotten home from school when the Social Worker pulled into the driveway. She stepped out of her car and walked around to the back door. From where I was standing, I could see someone in the backseat. The Social Worker opened the door and took the hands of 2 dark-complexioned boys. She led them into the house. They were approximately 3 and 4 years old. They were very shy and seemed extremely scared. The social worker told Mom that the younger boy's name was Juelio and the older was Pabloe. They hung on to each other, and tears were building up in their eyes. Mom bent down and tried to reassure them that they were safe.

I could not be sure if they understood what she was trying to tell them. They seemed to be more comfortable with Susie and me. Mom and the Social Worker led the boys into the living room and sat them on the sofa. The two boys came over to Susie and me while we were sitting in a large armchair nearby.

Mom then asked what the problem was with the two boys and why they were placed in foster care.

The social worker got up and walked over to where the boys were sitting. She took Pabloe's hand and turned him around so his back was towards Mom. She pulled his shirt out of his pants and very carefully pulled it up. I was in shock, and I could see that Mom was surprised and upset by what she saw, too. From the top of his back, close to his neck, all the way down to his butt crack, there was a large black scab, that fill his whole back from side to side.

Mom asked, "How did this happen?"

She was told by the social worker that his mom was upset because he soiled his pants and poured scalding hot water down his back.

The social worker told Mom, "This will take time to heal, and his mental health depends on how she works with him."

That first night, both boys were very restless, and Mom spent half the night trying to get them to go to sleep. She was given some lotion that had to be applied to Pabloe's back twice daily. He resisted Mom's touch at first and cried a lot. Mom would talk to him in a soft, calm voice, and after a few days, her voice seemed to calm him down. She took special care when applying the lotion. A bath was out of the question for either boy. Until Pabloe's scab fell off and his back was healed.

Juelio also had a fear of water. Mom took her time and bathed both boys almost every night. Pabloe was also deadly afraid of water of any kind. Just handing him a glass of water seemed to scare him. He would stick a finger in it to see if it was hot. Mom knew this would be a problem when it came for him to take a bath in a bathtub.

In a few weeks, the scab fell off, and his back no longer needed the lotion. It was time to introduce him to the bathtub. She only placed a few inches of water in the tub while undressing him. She lifted him and tried to get him to sit in the water.

He started to scream, "HOT" "HOT" "HOT" and pulled his legs up to his chest. Mom set him back onto the floor and told him to feel the water with his hands. He bent down, placing his hand in the water, and realized the water was not hot. Mom again picked him up and tried to put him in, and he slowly straightened his legs so his toes felt the water. He stood in the water for a few minutes and gradually sat down. Mom was so happy, she did it, and his mental health would now start healing.

Seeing his older brother enjoying the bathwater made Juelio join him in the tub as well. Both of the boys sat in the water and played for a while. Never again did Mom have a problem with the boys taking a bath. Water was no longer an issue for either of them. Watching mom take care of the two boys led me to understand her need for not only one but many children. She had a large, nurturing side that needed to be unleashed.

Grandmother saw this need in her at an early age, but she had no idea it would manifest into a house full of children, animals, maybe, but not children. I knew Dad was always unsure about their decision to take in more than one child but Mom always seemed so excited when the social worker would call and say she had another child who needed a home.

Dad said once that he never knew who would be sitting at the supper table when he came home from work in the evening. He would always scan around the table, searching for a strange face looking back at him.

The two foster brothers, Juelio and Pabloe

Meal Time

Mom did all of the cooking two to three times a day. Breakfast was always either toast or Cereal. One day, when I was nine years old, I came down the steps for breakfast before leaving for the bus stop. Once in a while, I would have toast with sugar and cinnamon. This was a day I will never forget. I made my own toast, sprinkling it with some sugar and cinnamon on top and then downed both slices.

Within approximately fifteen minutes, I got so sick and had to throw up a few times, but it did not last long, and soon after, I was on my way to school. For the next thirty years or so, I could not look at cinnamon or eat it without feeling sick. Mom only had to make lunch for the younger boys who had not gone to school yet. The rest of us had our lunch at school. She would make a light lunch consisting of soup with a piece of buttered bread or a sandwich with a cup of milk. No one ever went hungry.

Supper was a different story. Most of the time, Mom would make a large meal in the evening, and this is when all of us would be around the table. Mom never used a measuring cup or spoon. She would make large meals, pot roast, spaghetti, roast chicken, turkey, with mashed potatoes and two or three different kinds of vegetables. She seemed to have the knack of just throwing ingredients together and coming out with a terrific meal.

At times, money was a little tight, and Mom had to be creative in what to make for supper. Mom and Dad would try to save money any way they could. Once every two weeks, Dad would go to the Maier's Bakery and buy day-old Bread. The bakery had an outlet store where day-old items were sold. There were items like donuts, buns, and a few different types of bread. Dad would get approximately fifteen to twenty loaves of bread and a few other goodies. At the store, bread in the nineteen fifties was going for approximately fifteen cents per loaf. Dad could get the same items for approximately twelve cents each. They had no nutritional value, but were filling. A few cents saved may not seem much now, but back then, every penny counted.

I can remember one cold winter night in January, Mom could not get to the store. She made a large pot of cocoa. The kitchen table was approximately twelve feet long by three feet wide, with a long bench on each side and a chair at each end. Dad's place at the table was always on the one side, right in the middle. Mom would sit at the head of the table. Mom had all the small kids sit on either side of her, where she could serve them. Dad, sitting in the middle, could serve all of the other kids sitting at the far end of the table.

59

The large pot of cocoa sat in front of Dad, right in the middle of the table. He would serve all the cocoa, while Mom spread all the butter bread. The bread was passed down to the lower end of the table until everyone had at least two slices. Mom was sure the cocoa was not too hot for the smaller kids. As everyone dipped their butter bread and ate, Mom watched to be sure everyone left the table full. If needed, we all could have more cocoa and bread.

Some meals only consisted of corn on the cob or strawberries with little angel food cakes. Every Wednesday was payday for Dad, and Mom would make a weekly trip to the store. We could always count on bologna sandwiches and soda for supper. When mom did not want to cook, dad would go for hot dogs. There was a place about six miles from the house where Dad could get hot dogs for ten cents each. One of us would go with him, and he would order thirty to forty hot dogs. It only cost him around four to five dollars, and he had enough to feed everyone.

At least once a month, on a Sunday evening, Dad would go to Shillington to a small store on Lancaster Avenue. Here, he would buy four to five one-half gallons of ice cream. He would always get at least one Chocolate marshmallow, 2 Vanilla, and one that had three flavors.

Susie, Dad, and I would always get some of the Chocolate marshmallow. Dad loved his chocolate. The Ice cream came in a cardboard box. Dad would open the carton from all sides, and all that lay on the table was a large square cube of ice cream. He would then take a large knife, not a scoop, and cut a two- to three-inch-thick slice for each of us. This was only a small example of how Mom and Dad showed us that even when times were hard, love and our faith would put food on the table.

Mom was a great cook; she could throw things together without measuring. Her specialty was chocolate pies with a meringue topping. She would use coconut and egg whites. No matter what mom whipped up, it always tasted like a professional chef made it. There were no frills of a five-star restaurant, but it tasted much better. I never learned to cook from my mom since she had no recipe to follow, only what was in her head. I cannot say how she learned to cook, was from watching her mom or from the years she spent with Nanna.

She had the know-how to make enough for a large family with little leftovers. Planning meals for a week for so many was not easy. I never saw Mom with a store list when she went shopping. She knew what she needed and filled her cart for the week, and she never did any canning or put up preserves. You would think, living during the depression, she would have learned this skill. Making supper for a large family took more than what Mom could do herself, so Dad would assist her in getting the food ready, like mashing the potatoes and carving the meat. Being a tomboy, I never had any interest in learning to cook.

Tom Boys

The only life that Susie and I ever knew from the day we were born was that of living in Cedar Top. A community on top of a mountain. There were only a few distant neighbors. People were starting to build on this mountain. A large field was in the back of the house, and a large wooded area was on the front. Susie and I were growing up with a house full of boys.

During the years when we were only seven, eight, and nine years old, we shared a lot of the activities the boys would do. Playing in the field and the woods was our main playground. The boys never bothered us, knowing we were girls, as far as they cared, we were just one of the boys.

Mom and Dad did not seem to worry about us playing with the boys. One day, Mom bought all of us some toy cap guns. We also got a few boxes of firecrackers that we would place in the guns to make the guns sound like shots when the triggers were pulled. It did not take long to fire them. Telling Mom and Dad that we used all the fire crackers, they would buy us more. We would run through the field, hiding among the large boulders in the woods, playing cowboys and Indians.

Boulders in the woods were huge, so climbing on them was fun. On the back side of the woods was a trash dump. We would rummage through the dump to see what goodies we could find. Most of the items were badly rusted or broken. Every once in a while, we would find something we could use in our fort that we had built.

Building a fort was important in fighting off the Indians. We would use whatever we could find to build a fort or even a tree house. Even though we were very young, we had some basic skills in building. Dad would give us whatever wood and nails he had left from a project to upgrade our fort. Owning a house meant there were many repairs to be done.

Sledding

Mom and Dad made sure that every season left us wanting more. Sure, the winter months brought in the Christmas season, but there was so much more to it for the kids living in "The Hen House."

In winters, living on top of a mountain, there was always plenty of snow. Sleigh riding was a big part of my memories. There were about five kids, including Susie and me, who were old enough to go sleigh riding on their own during the day, and at night when it was pitch dark. Mom and Dad would take the smaller kids out during the daylight hours. They made sure that no one was left out.

During the day, we would have to share our sleds with the younger kids. We had no problem with this, since they would not stay out too long. The weather was much too cold for them. At night, we each had our own sleds, with our names on them, that we got for Christmas either last year or this year. We would sit and watch the snow accumulate during the day, just waiting for it to be deep enough to go out.

Sometimes school interfered with our sleigh riding during the day, but there was always the nighttime. We would come home after school and do our homework before being allowed to go out. Down in the cellar were hooks where our winter sleigh-riding clothes would hang. On the floor was a lineup of rubber boots. During these early years, no one had a snowsuit, so to keep warm, our snow clothes would consist of two to three pairs of pants, two to three sweaters worn under a heavy snow jacket with a hat and a hood. The gloves we had worn were made out of cotton, so they got wet very quickly. To help keep our hands warm, we would place one or two pairs of socks under the gloves or mittens.

I recall when we wanted the snow to freeze like ice. To accomplish this, a few boys went out after school and used the water hose to wet the snow. Two older boys started at the top of the hill and sprinkled the water as far down as the hose would reach. By the time Homework was done, and the sun was going down, the water on the hill would be freezing and would be very icy.

Gathering our clothes in the basement, we all got dressed. It took a while to get all the clothes on. I remember how difficult it was putting on two boots, with all the bulky clothes on. It was so hard to bend down and buckle them. The boots worn would go over a pair of shoes, so we could not wear heavy socks. Each boot had five buckles. You had to put one side of the buckle over the front of the boot into the slot on the other side and lock it down.

Once I was dressed, I grabbed my American Flyer Sled and opened the door to leave the cellar when a cold blast of air hit me right on my face. Stepping onto the snow, I could hear it crunch beneath my feet as I walked towards the hill. The air was crisp and cold. The winds would blow through the trees from the woods and come right across the path we have made for our sleds. With every gust of wind, I could feel my face and nose getting colder and colder. Taking a deep breath was somewhat painful as the cold would go deep into my lungs. I would cover my mouth with a scarf to prevent my lips from chapping. My cheeks would get fire engine red, while my glasses would fog up with every breath I took.

Looking up the ice-covered hill filled me with anticipation. I was the second person out of the cellar, knowing the rest were not far behind. Walking to the top of the hill, right out in front of the house, took only a few minutes, but with the wind and the cold, it seemed like a mile. The moonlit sky and the faint light emanating from the house were enough to see down the hill. The path the sleds would travel disappeared into pure darkness, which was a little scary; it was like entering a dark tunnel, and you were never sure what was at the other end. Placing my sled on the snow, I gave a small push. I flopped down on my stomach and off I went.

The snow froze solid, and it was more ice than snow. The sled went approximately one hundred feet down the hill before it hit the driveway.

There were another hundred feet to the main road. I can only guess, but I believe it to be one quarter of a mile. There was only one drawback to this great ride down the hill: knowing we had a long walk back up to do it again. Since the snow on the road was packed down, it was as slippery as the hill where the water was applied, also turning it into ice, so just walking was a challenge. Susie and I would stay out until we could no longer take the cold.

When we could no longer feel our fingers or toes, we would go into the cellar and remove all our sleigh riding clothes, one piece at a time. We would then go upstairs to warm up. It would take a few minutes to remove the layers of clothes. What made it so difficult was that our pants would have snow caked and would be frozen to the cuffs. The boots were the worst to remove because snow and ice would be packed into every buckle. Since the gloves would not keep our hands warm, by the time we came in, our hands were so cold that we could barely feel them. A few times, we yelled for Dad to come down and help us unhook the buckles. Mom would fix us some hot chocolate to warm up our insides, and wrap our feet in a warm towel.

We would stay in the house for a short time, warming up. Our fingers and toes had barely thawed out when it was time to go in the cellar, put on our wet outer clothes, and go sleigh riding some more. I hardly had time for the redness to leave my cheeks and to get the feeling back into my hands and feet. We could do this up to three times in an evening, starting at around five pm, an hour and a half out, and an hour in.

Some nights on weekends, we would be sleigh riding up to 11 pm. Some days, I would get tired of getting dressed and undressed, but who could resist the fun? I do not know what the draw was, for not only me, but for the rest of the kids, to keep defying the cold and doing it again. Rushing home from school one day to go sleigh riding, Susie and I were walking up the driveway when we noticed in the distance, a large snowman standing on the front lawn. As we got closer, we could see that it was pretty nice. Someone knew how to build a snowman.

As we entered the house, we asked Mom, "Who rolled the balls for the snowman?"

She told us that she got the small boys all dressed in snow clothes and took them out for a while.

She said, "The boys pitched in and helped roll the large snowballs for his body. It was a problem trying to lift the two larger ones, but we managed."

Since she did not have any coal, she had to dig under the snow in the driveway to look for five small rocks to place on his stomach and two for his eyes. While the boys continued to play in the snow, she went inside to look for an old scarf and a hat. The scarf was not hard to find, but the hat was a different story. She went through all the drawers and shelves looking for the right one. She looked for a while, all the time keeping a watch on the boys still outside. She found an old hat that Dad wore when they were dating. It was dusty and had a few moth holes, but it would work perfectly. The hat was a solid black felt fabric. Mom was uncertain how long it would hold up in the weather, day and night. The red and black scarf wrapped around the neck of the snowman twice.

Mom stood back and could tell that something was missing. Then it came to her, how could she forget his nose? She went right back into the house to the refrigerator to get a carrot. She was unsure how large a carrot she should use for the nose since the bag had a variety of sizes. She took the whole bag outside with her to select the right one.

As the kids arrived home from school, they admired her hard work. It was time for all of the kids to go. Mom undressed all the smaller kids and said it was time for her to start supper. She said 'Homework had to be done if we wanted to go sleigh riding.' Mom whipped up a fast meal, and with lightning speed, we were in the basement putting on our snow clothes. The winters in the mid-

1950s were so much fun.

Valentines Day

Valentine's Day was not as big of a deal as some of the larger holidays during the year. For some reason, no one ever mentioned this to Mom. A week before, she would start decorating the house with red hearts. To do this, she would sit at the kitchen table with the younger kids and have them draw and cut out hearts. To make it more interesting, she would not use colored Crayons, but instead brought out the water colors. She figured they always played with crayons, but were not allowed to use watercolors without supervision.

She did not forget the older kids, like Susie and me. She managed to get to the store and buy a shopping cart full of Valentine cards. These came in large boxes of approximately twenty cards per box. She would give the older kids up to two boxes. She knew there were approximately thirty kids in each of their classes. I don't think Valentine's Day has been celebrated in schools this way for years. Each kid would sit at the kitchen table and make out their cards, making sure to give one to each classmate, whether they liked them or not. After all, this was the time to love everyone.

The next day at school, we would pass out all of our cards and receive a card from each classmate. Some of the cards showed love, while some were comical. Though mom had the craftsmanship to do Valentine's Day. The month of February had come to an end, and the month of March was Dad's time to take over.

Flying Kites

As the winter winds and the cold, blowing snow were in the past months, we all looked forward to Spring. The weather was warming up during the day, but the nights were still pretty cold. We all heard the old saying, "The March winds bring in the April showers that bring in the May flowers."

It was time to begin the outside fun. We would wait every day during March for Dad to come home with the kites, just like every year. Spring was in the air, the daffodil and the spring flowers were starting to break through the defrosting earth. We knew from the previous year that the large field in the back of the house was the best place to fly kites. Each year, around mid-March, the farmer who owned the field would come through with a large mower and cut down all the brush. We would watch the mower go back and forth, knowing it was soon time to get the kites. Each day that passed, more birds were flying around, and the air was fresher.

Every day after school, we would wait for dad to see if he stopped and got the kites, or must we wait another day? The day did finally come, and as Dad got out of his car, we saw that he was holding a large bag. All of the kids would follow Dad into the house, where he laid the kites on the sofa. We would have to wait until after supper for Dad to hand out the kites. Only the eight-year-olds and older kids received a kite. As he emptied the bag on the sofa, large rolls of white kite string would fall out. He handed each of us two rolls. The smaller kids, Dad would take under his wings, and be sure they all had a turn to fly a kite.

When Supper was over and all the dishes were washed and put away. It was time for Dad to pass out the kites. He emptied the bag onto the table, and as each kid picked out their kite, Dad reminded them how fragile they were. The sticks that made up the kites were extremely thin, and the paper could tear very easily. The boys each took their kites to their rooms, where they attempted to put them together. In most cases, Dad was called in to assist. These kites were very simple to put together, but the bending of the sticks took a little finesse.

Once in a while, Dad would also break one, but he made sure to buy a few extra just in case. While dad and the kids were working on their kites, mom was rummaging around the house for some old rags to make tails for all the kites. Tying thin strips of rags together and connecting them to the bottom of a kite gives stability to the kite as it is flying. Without a tail, a kite would start spinning in a circle and crash to the ground.

Once the farmer had finished mowing the field, it was ready

for us to launch our kites.

By the time we got all the kites together, it would be too late to go out and fly them. We would have to wait until the next day after school to see if they would fly. The only safe place to store a kite was under each bed. When we arrived home from school the following day, Dad came home early and was waiting for us. We all grabbed our kites and headed up to the field. Before launching our kites, we had to attach the string and then look for a proximally twelve-inch-long round stick. The string was on a roll, with a hole in the center. We would place the stick into the hole and place a hand on each side. Laying the kite on the ground and letting out some of the string, we could now walk up to where the kite was lying. We were now ready to get the kite in the sky.

As one person picked up the stick and held on to it, the other person ran with the kite in tow. As soon as the kite was up in the air, around ten feet, the person holding on to the stick would start running while letting out more string. If everything went ok, the kite would slowly climb higher and higher. Watching the string go out was so important. The higher the kite went, the string on the roll would come to an end. If the string ran out before you could grab the end, the kite would fly away and be lost forever. It would fly too far away to retrieve it or end up in a tree. The trick was to hold on to the kite while another person tied the second string to the first. It would have to be tied securely or the kite would fly away.

Once the kite was in the air, I would lie on the ground, which was still a little cold from the winter thaw. The only smell was that of the freshly cut field. The aroma would fill my head with a soothing feeling of peace. As I got older, the smell of freshly cut grass would take me back to that peaceful time. I could lie there for hours just watching the kite wave back and forth with the wind.

My kite would travel so high that it would look like a tiny dot among the clouds. The quietness left me time to daydream and forget about the world around me. I would look around and see that there were kites that were still lying on the ground. Dad was trying his best to get to everyone who needed his help. It took an hour or so to get everyone's kite in the air, but Dad did it. Lying, looking up, and watching 6 to 7 kites gliding with the wind was beautiful. Dad would circle to check on each of us to be sure we did not need his help. We were all close enough to each other, so if anyone needed help, a loud yell would do. I felt Dad was enjoying flying the kites more than the kids. He felt the excitement each kid had when their kite left the ground. The expression on each face gave him the energy to go on. I knew he was tired after working all day, but he never showed it.

He was like the little engine that could last so long, or the

Energizer Bunny. Mom would come out of the house every few minutes to see how Dad was doing. If he needed her help, she would be there for him. Mom would walk the two smaller boys to the field where Dad watched the kites. He stood behind one of the small boys and handed him the stick with the kite string on. He bent down and whispered to the boy to hold on tight. The expression on his face was priceless.

After a few minutes, he handed the stick to the second boy and waited for his reaction. Dad knew that everyone would go to bed that night with the experience of flying a kite to dream of. Flying a kite was something that Dad never had a chance to do. Life for him on the farm was strict, and the farm work came before any leisure time. Seeing the sky full of kites just weaving around was beautiful; it looked like a rainbow of all different colors.

After a while, Dad would come and tell us that it was time to bring down the kites, the sun was going down. Dad knew it would take some time to bring down all of the kites. The worst part of flying a kite was standing there and wrapping the string around the stick as you brought it down. My hands would get tired and my wrists would hurt, but I could not wait for the next day to do it again.

Easter

Once the March winds had passed, it was mid-April. Rain showers were in the forecast nightly. It was time to open all the windows and let the fresh spring air flow throughout the house. It was time for the flowers to break through the ground, and for the Easter Bunny to show off his two long ears and a basket full of candy.

Mom and Dad loved Easter. A few days before Easter, Mom would make 2 to 3 dozen hard-boiled eggs, and Susie and I would help Mom decorate them. We both loved spending this time with her. Easter mornings were special. Mom prepared each of us a beautiful Easter basket full of candy. The baskets would be placed in the living room, waiting for us to discover them in the morning.

Mom would hide the eggs that we decorated all around the house. Before checking out the baskets, we would have to find all the eggs. When Susie and I were 6 years old, Mom loved dressing everyone up for Easter. She bought Susie and me a beautiful Easter dress and a wide-brimmed bonnet, with white patent leather shoes. Nelson would be decked out in a black suit. Dad did not like suits, so he would wear a new pair of dress pants and just a dress shirt.

Mom was so different; she loved dressing up in a beautiful mid-length dress and a small hat that sat on the top of her head. After taking many pictures of everything, Mom would start the large Easter dinner. She would make a large ham, with mashed potatoes and two to three types of vegetables. Mom made sure that we did not eat too much candy before dinner. We placed the baskets in our bedrooms. If mom or dad saw us eating too much candy, they would take the basket away from us for a while.

Years later, after the house was full of kids, Easter did not change that much. Mom would let the smaller boys decorate the eggs. She would still make up Easter baskets for all of us. She had to get creative since there were many more baskets to make. She did not have the money to buy woven baskets, so she used shoe boxes. She would place the Easter grass in all the boxes and fill each with an assortment of candy. The shoe boxes were placed in the living room, with each having a name on it. I recall one Easter when the house was full of kids and candy. You only had two choices: either you ate the candy fast, or you hid it. The younger kids would sneak into our room and help themselves to it.

One day before going to bed, I thought I would be smart; I placed my box behind the radiator in my room. Forgetting the nights would still get cold, and the heater would go on, well, you can guess what happened. In the morning, I woke up to a lump of green grass with candy melted into it. With tears in my eyes, I ended up throwing it all away. Needless to say, I learned a huge lesson that Easter.

Sharing a little is better than having nothing to share. Susie felt so bad for me that she offered to share whatever candy she had left. This is what sisters do.

Those Summer Days

Summer was slowly coming, and school would soon be over for the year. The weather was getting much warmer, so the winter clothes were going away and the shorts were coming out. Susie and I both passed to the next grade and, like every year, would attend a new class in the fall.

Now that we were a bit older, playing cowboys and Indians in the woods was no longer what we wanted to do. We were looking forward to going down to the Mohnton playground. This was another community down the mountain, about 2 miles from our house. The only way to get to the playground was to walk or ride a bike. We were young, so the walk did not bother us; it was the walk back up the mountain that took the wind out of our sails. As much as we hated the walk home, we did it day after day with no complaints.

There was so much to do at the playground. There were many sports, games and activities, from baseball, four corners, hockey, and basketball. Under the pavilion, there were crafts and board games. Sitting at the wooden picnic tables, we had our choice of activities. There were instructors to help us with the crafts. There were swings, see-saws, sliding boards, and a merry-go-round. We would spend hours and hours just going from one activity to another. Mom always made sure that we had something to drink. The instructors at the playground would have water and lemonade

Dad holding Susie and me right after our birth in 1949

for all the kids.

Mom wanted to be sure we had some refreshments in case the instructors were not there, so she would give us each a dime. At the far end of the playground was a small gas station. Here we could use our dimes to get a bottle of Coke.

We would spend hours playing and doing crafts. Without a watch or clock, we always knew when the time had come to make that long hike up the mountain. Mom made sure we understood that we had to be home by suppertime. If we came home late, we would not be allowed to go to the playground for a week. We all arrived home at different times but were never late for supper.

During this time, Mom and Dad had around five boys aged five to ten years. Only the older boys over 8 were allowed to go to the playground. Mom and Dad could always come up with a surprise for all of us, no matter what day it was.

One day, as we were all at the playground, Mom and Dad pulled up in the car. All I could think of was that we did something wrong or what we forgot. As we ran around to find the rest of the boys to tell them that Mom and Dad were here, they too wondered what was wrong. We all approached the car in anticipation.

Mom rolled down the window and told us, "All to get in."

It was a very hot summer day, and we were going swimming. The only place to go swimming without belonging to a public pool was a place called Cross Keys. This was about fifteen miles from home, along Route 61 in Maiden Creek Township. Turning off Route 61 was a long metal bridge crossing the Schuylkill River.

On the far side of the bridge, on the left, was a small parking area. Dad pulled in, and we all got out of the car. Since we were picked up at the playground, none of us had on our swimming suits. Dad took the boys a short distance from the car while Mom opened the back door on the far side. Throwing a blanket over the doors made the windows hard to see through.

Mom helped Susie and me undress and put on our swimming suits. In a few minutes, Susie and I were dressed, and we would start down the hill to the river. In the meantime, Dad would stay behind and help the boys put on their swimming trunks. It did not take long for the boys to change their clothes. Before we knew it, they were right behind us, climbing down the hill. This was not an easy task, since the hill was full of large river rocks and boulders.

Looking up at the large metal bridge, I watched cars crossing it in both directions. The roadway was all wooden planks, so I had no need to see a car to know there was one on the bridge.

Mom did not go in the water, and since Dad was not a strong swimmer, he made sure he could stand in the deepest part. There was only a small area where the water was calm. Getting too close to the bridge's cement pillar would mean getting into the rapids.

Entering the water was slow. It was cold and I could not see the bottom. There were tiny rocks on the bottom that could hurt the bottom of my feet. Not knowing how deep it was, I took my time, taking tiny steps. I was afraid it would just drop off and I would go under. I had a pair of goggles that I used to see under the water. I swear, at times, I could feel something brush against my legs. I would put on the goggles and put my face in the water. I am not sure what I would have done if I saw a fish swim by.

I saw different-sized rocks and long blades of grass swaying with the current. Dad would tease us by saying he saw a large fish. For some reason, I did not feel threatened by anything that could have been in the water. Dad was there to make sure we were all safe.

During one of these trips to the river, Dad plucked me out of the water, threw me a short distance, and said, "Swim."

Guess what? I did. Knowing I could swim gave me all the confidence I needed to feel safe in any body of water. From that time on, my swimming skills improved. Swimming is one activity that I enjoyed for the rest of my life. Leaving the rocky beach to go back to the car was treacherous. Since we all had wet feet, slipping off the rocks was always on our minds. Thank God, there were never any injuries to any of us.

Arriving back at the car, Mom would take Susie and me aside and, behind the car doors to change back into our dry clothes. Dad did the same with the boys. Arriving home at around 5:00 in the evening was too late for Mom to make supper. Anticipating this, Mom had gone to the store while we were at the playground. Bologna Sandwiches were on the menu that night. Then, it was time to take a shower and go to bed. I was so tired and my skin felt hot. I know by morning I would be red.

A few years later, going to the swimming hole at Cross Keys was no longer an option. To keep track of all the kids in a river would not be safe. Mom and Dad decided to put in an in-ground swimming pool. I overheard them talking and could not believe my ears, a swimming pool, wow! I would not dare say anything, or mom and dad would know I was eavesdropping. I kept it to myself for a few days, until one evening at the supper table, the subject came up, and the cat was out of the bag.

Swimming Pool

Mom and Dad made their decision, and knew it was time to let the kids in on the news.

Mom said, "We are putting in a swimming pool in the backyard."

The expression on the kids' faces as I looked around the table was one of surprise.

They looked at each other and said, "Really, a swimming pool?"

Mom said, "Yes, an inground swimming pool."

Winter was coming, and it was too late to start on a pool until spring. Waiting a few months would also give them a little time to save some money. A Swimming pool was a large undertaking for Mom and Dad. They wanted to give the family more than just a trip to a small place under a bridge to cool off and play in the water, but they never had the space to learn how to swim.

When one of the boys heard that Dad was going to dig a hole to put in a swimming pool, he grabbed a shovel from the basement, went out in the yard, and started to dig the hole.

Foster boy digging a hole for the swimming pool

Dad told him that it would take more than he could do alone to dig a large enough hole. Knowing we were getting a pool made the winter months go so slowly. Every month, we were all anticipating when the construction would begin.

Dad said that he had to wait until the ground had started to thaw out. It was late March when Dad made the call for the bulldozer. It was another week until the bulldozer arrived. We were all in school and did not know that the digging of the hole had begun. By the time we got home, there was a pile of dirt on the side of the road. A large hole was in the yard. Dad was inside the hole, measuring the depth and the length. Dad asked the bulldozer operator to pile the dirt along the edge of the hole and smooth it out. The hole was now ready for the cinder blocks. In the late 1950s, swimming pools did not have liners. A liner would have made it easier for Dad.

He had a truckload of cinder blocks ordered and delivered to the house. It seemed like Dad's work was never done. First, it was the house addition, and now a pool. Every weekend, Dad and Mom's brother Tom would work laying the cinder blocks, constructing the walls for the pool. It took a few days to finish the walls, and now it was time to lay the floor.

Dad had to make another phone call for a truckload of sand and cement. During the week, Dad and Tom shoveled the sand into the hole and smoothed it out. The following weekend, the cement truck arrived and started pouring it. We all stood and watched the cement roll down a large chute into the bottom of the pool. As the cement entered the pool, Dad was on the bottom, smoothing it out. Once the floor was laid and the cement had dried, Dad and Tom had to do the same with the walls. Dad had to have a water filtering unit installed.

A pipe had to be put in, which went from the filter under the ground and into the side wall of the pool. This unit was to keep the water clean and safe for swimming. Watching day after day, just waiting for the weather to warm up enough to swim in the new pool was like waiting for the man on the moon to say hello.

Every day, we inched closer and closer to putting on our swimming suits. It took a few weeks for the cement to dry before water could start flowing into it. Mom wanted the inside of the pool to be painted blue. Tom's wife painted a beautiful mermaid on the floor of the deep end. After months of anticipation, the day we were all waiting for finally arrived.

Dad went to the back side of the house and pulled the garden hose out, placing the end into the pool. He turned on the water, and slowly the pool was filling. Living out in the woods, there was no public water system; we only had a water well that grandfather had dug when dad built the house. Since we only had a well, the pump could not be run for too long, or it might burn out. Dad would only let it run a few hours a day. Every day after school, I checked on the water level in the pool. When full, it would be six feet deep at the deepest end, and only three feet deep at the shallow end. Mom wanted to be sure that Dad could stand in the deepest part. The weather during the day was still too cold to go swimming, and school had not yet ended. We all knew that even if the pool were full, it would take a few weeks of the summer sun to warm it up.

Standing on the rim of the pool, I stared into the water. I was amazed to see that the beautiful mermaid seemed to be moving. Watching her tail and her hair waving with the movement of the water gave me an eerie feeling. I could not wait to jump and swim to the bottom of the pool to see her up close and in person. For some reason, even though she looked scary, I was not afraid.

When the filter was in place, Dad's next job was to cement the walkway around the total edge of the pool. Since Dad had the bulldozer driver smooth out all the dirt he removed from the hole, it was easier for him to get the walkway laid. Once Dad had the dirt in place, the dirt needed to be covered with cement. Dragging all of this dirt into the pool was not an option.

While Dad was finishing the walkway around the rim of the pool, Uncle Tom was installing a wooden 8-foot fence around the outer side of the walkway. Mom wanted this done as soon as possible. The pool was full of water, and she was worried a neighbor kid would fall into it. Again, this would be another delay before we could go swimming. It took at least another two weeks for the cement to dry, get the filter running, finish filling the pool, and have the sun warm the water. It was now mid-June, and school was over for the year.

The wooden 8-foot fence around the outer side of the pool

One very warm day, Mom told us it was time to test out the new pool. She had us all put on our swimming suits. Mom was the first one to jump into the water. Even though she was still very heavy, she dove into the water like an Olympic diver.

She came to the top of the water, gasping and said, "The water is still very cold, but if you guys want to come in, you can."

The smaller kids sat on the edge, dangling their feet in the cold water. Susie and I, feeling brave, stood on the rim of the deep end and just jumped in.

As we hit the water, it took our breath away. As soon as we came up from under the water, we headed for the steps. As much as we could not wait to get into the pool, we now could not wait to get out. We did this a few times, jumping in and getting out right away.

Once our bodies got used to the coldness of the water, we could stay in longer and longer. The time came for me to swim the six feet to the bottom of the deep end of the pool to check out the mermaid. I took one deep breath and down I went. Swimming around the bottom, I could see her up close and how beautiful she was. As I was taking in her beauty, I saw Susie right next to me, again sharing experiences is what twins do. We swam around for a few more seconds, and without knowing, we both popped back up to the surface at the same time, wiping the water from our faces.

Susie said, "Do you want to do it again?"

I said, "Sure," and down into the deep we went again.

One of our favorite things to do was to jump into the cold water, get out right away, run very slowly around the pool two or three times, and then jump back in. Dripping with water as we left the pool and not having a towel to wrap in, we were cold. After a few times around the pool, we would jump back in. The air on the outside cooled our bodies, so when we jumped back into the water, it seemed very warm.

<u>Susie and me standing by the pool, 1960</u>

Mom would take one of the smaller boys and walk him around the pool, making sure he was not scared of the water. Remember, the two small boys, Pabloe and Juelio, with Mom's care, were no longer afraid of water and were jumping into Mom's arms as she stood in the pool. I could see the satisfying look on Mom's face, knowing this was all due to her love and patience.

Putting in a pool was one of the best things Mom and Dad could have done. We always looked forward to summers, and we spent many days and evenings just playing in the water. Going on a vacation was never an issue for us. Between the playground, the pool, and all the activities, Mom and Dad would do with us filled up our summers. This is not saying that we did not go on day trips. The one trip that we took was to Dorney Park.

Foster boys hanging on the edge of the swimming pool

Dorney Park

Dorney Park was only a small amusement park in the late 1950s. It was the only park within driving distance from Berks County. One day, Mom and Dad told us that we would spend a whole day at the park. I can't tell you how excited we all were.

I had heard about the large roller coaster at the park, but I never dreamed a day would come when I would ride it.

Early in the morning, Mom and Dad got up with the chickens. All of the kids were still sleeping. The night before, Mom had placed a few containers of water in the freezer to make ice. Dad got the large metal cooler from the basement. Mom sat at the kitchen table and made everyone two bologna sandwiches. Mom wrapped all the sandwiches and placed them in the cooler.

Dad, meanwhile, was making a large container of Kool-Aid. He then placed it into the cooler under some of the ice. Mom packed a large canvas bag full of treats like cookies and fruit. There was no need for flatware since we only had sandwiches to eat. Mom grabbed a large number of plastic cups from the cabinet.

Now that everything was ready, it was time for them to wake us up. We were so excited and hurried to get dressed. Mom was getting the bowls and cereal out so we could have breakfast before leaving. They wanted to leave around ten thirty in the morning. We all had some chores to finish before leaving, like making the beds, washing the breakfast dishes, and seeing that the two smaller boys were dressed.

There were Susie and I, Nelson, and five foster boys. At this time, Dad owned a Station wagon. Dad and Nelson went out to tie the cooler to the car roof. There was just enough room for everyone in the car. Three boys sat in the back seat, looking out the back of the car. Susie, Nelson, and I sat in the second seat, and the two small boys sat upfront with mom and dad. We were now all ready to go.

Dad locked up the house, and away we went. It would take at least one and a half hours to get to Allentown, where the park was located. When we were only a few miles away from the park, Dad pulled off the road to a large wooden picnic table. This table sat down a small hill and was a little dirty. Mom spread a large cloth onto the table while Dad and Nelson untied the cooler from the top of the car. Mom and Dad had very little money and could not afford food at the park. They only had so much money to buy us all ride tickets. We all sat down and had lunch before continuing to the park.

It was now close to noon, and the park had been open for an

hour or so.

As we approached the park, Dad said, "Look out the window, do you see the roller coaster?"

I cannot speak for everyone else, but I was so excited pulling into the parking lot. Standing on the hill above the park, I saw the roller coaster up close. It was just coming down the very high hill, and the sound was deafening. Dad and Nelson again took the cooler off the roof of the car, and it still had Cool-Aid and snacks in it. We all walked down the hill, and Dad placed the cooler on a wooden picnic table under the roller coaster. The two smaller boys stayed with Mom while Dad went to a ticket booth and bought a large roll of ride tickets. We stayed with Mom, waiting for Dad to return with the tickets. It only took a few minutes for him to buy the tickets and return to where we were waiting. He handed everyone a handful of tickets and told us to return within two hours or whenever we had no more tickets left. We were told to meet back at the one picnic table where they would be waiting for us.

Susie and I were allowed to go out on our own. Nelson went one way, and Susie and I went another. The three older foster boys could also go out on their own. Even though we all went in different directions, we all ended up at the large wooden roller coaster.

I was just at the park this past summer, 2024. It was nothing like it was back when I was a small girl. Susie and I could go on ride after ride with no long lines. Now, we were there for four hours and only got on two of three rides. We had to be picky, choosing the rides we wanted to get on. Waiting in line could take up to twenty minutes to an hour to get on one ride. The cost to get into both parks was out of this world.

Life back when I was a small girl was so much simpler. The park was so much smaller, but the fun could last for hours. No waiting in lines, no overcrowded walkways, and no need to worry that you would get lost. The park was easy to navigate.

We all met at the picnic table under the roller coaster in plenty of time. Mom and Dad had taken the two small boys on the rides in the kiddie park. The two small boys sat at the table, eating an apple. Mom and Dad had gathered up all the trash and were ready for the long ride home. We all headed for the car that sat on the hill. The walk up was much harder than the walk down.

As we approached the car, I could not help taking one more look at the park and the large rollercoaster. I took my seat in the car and off we went. As dad was driving away, I knew, in the back of my mind, that this day would always stay with me. It is a memory I will never forget.

On the way home, all we could talk about was what rides we were on and our experience on each ride. As we arrived home, the sun was going down. I remember how tired I was and hoped someday, we could do it all over again. I also noticed that I did get a little sunburn and how red my skin was getting. Money may have been an issue, but life was never dull.

Rides in the County

There was never much money, so going on many trips was not in the budget. To get everyone out of the house, other than going swimming or to the playground, Mom and Dad would load us all up into the car and go for a ride. The station wagon was gone, and Dad had a four-door Pontiac sedan. Going anywhere as a family was a challenge.

Dad placed a three-foot-long bench behind the front seat. It sat over the hump on the floor. Susie and I would sit on each end of the bench while there were four kids on the seat and one in the middle of mom and dad on the front seat. Mom would hold the smallest boy on her lap. Dad would start driving, not knowing where he was going. He would drive around on backcountry roads he had never been on before.

We always asked him, "Are we lost? Do you know where we are?"

He would answer, "No, but do not worry, we will eventually come out on a road that I know. We cannot get lost."

After an hour or so, he would come out on a familiar road. Dad would drive for a while longer before heading back home.

On the way home, he would go up Lancaster Avenue to an ice cream shop called Snow Kiss. Dad would pull into the parking lot, and we would all get out of the car.

Dad would say, "Order any kind of ice cream you like."

There were a few picnic tables to sit at, or we could go sit in the car. Mom and Dad were never in a hurry, giving us plenty of time to sit and talk while eating our ice cream. Now that the sun had gone down, it was time to go home. Mom and Dad knew how to make a ride in the country feel like a day trip. We all seemed to enjoy just riding around and having ice cream. Mom and Dad tried to make a simple ride into an adventure. Mom saved a little money from Dad's pay each week, so they could afford to take us on many more rides or day trips. Every year, it seemed money was getting tighter and tighter.

One evening, while sitting at home, Mom suggested raising some chickens. She said, by raising chickens, we could collect the eggs and eat the older chickens.

Dad agreed to Mom's request. Dad raised chickens when he lived at home on the farm. He knew what was needed and told Mom he would pick up the lumber and wire in a week.

The Chicken Coop

It was about a week later, on a Saturday, that Dad started to build a chicken coop. He came home after work one day with some lumber and chicken wire.

Right after supper, Susie and I followed him to the backyard. He got all his tools out and started sawing the lumber for the coop. He had the floor finished by the time the sun went down. The following day was Saturday, so he had the whole day to work on the coop.

Susie and I watched and asked many questions: "Where is the door going to be, what are the long boards going across the coop for, and why was there a need for small baskets along the wall?"

Dad was very forthcoming in answering all of our questions.

He said, "The door would go on the side, and the long boards were for the chickens to sit on, and the boxes are where they will lay their eggs."

We stayed with him throughout the day, watching and asking many more questions. He said that he should be able to finish the coop the following day, which was Sunday. We knew that since it would be finished on Sunday, Dad could not get any baby chickens until Monday after work.

It was a very warm day in mid-August. Not only were Susie and I waiting for Dad to come home, but Mom seemed to be just as excited. She had the smaller boys dressed, and we were all waiting for Dad's arrival. We watched Dad's car turn onto the driveway as he slowly drove home.

Standing on the front yard, we watched Dad open the trunk and lift a large box of baby chicks. Standing not far away, we could hear all the baby chicks peeping. As Dad walked across the yard to the back of the house, we all followed closely. As dad approached the coop, we ran up to the side where the chicken wire was attached. Dad slowly opened the door to the coop and set the box inside.

As soon as he lifted off the lid, all of the baby chicks started jumping out. It was a wonderful sight to see. I never asked him if any of the chickens were roosters or not. I am not sure if he even knew. Dad knew that to add any young chickens to the coop, a few roosters were necessary, but for right now, he said, "For now, we will just wait and see."

The chicks were so cute and very tiny. I stood along the fence watching them running around inside the coop. Each morning at sunrise, Mom would go out and sprinkle some chicken feed around on the ground. It took a month or so before the chicks were old enough to lay eggs.

One day, I went out to check on the chicks, and I noticed something white in one of the boxes. I ran into the house and told Mom I believe the chickens have started to lay eggs. She went out with me, and sure enough, one tiny pure white egg was lying in one of the boxes. From that day on, every day we could count on a few fresh eggs for breakfast.

I knew that all the chickens had grown up, but one day I went out to check on them and to collect the eggs. I was shocked to see some baby chicks running around the outside of the pen. I ran to the house and told Mom and Dad what I had found. They both came out, and there, running around the outside of the pen, were approximately five tiny baby chicks.

Since the eggs were collected daily, we could not understand how they got out of the pen. As Dad looked around the pen, he saw a small hole in the wire where one of the chickens had gotten out. She then went under the coop and built herself a nest. This is where she hatched her eggs.

Dad said, "I guess that answers the question if there was a rooster among the chicks."

Now that some chickens were hatching baby chicks, the coop

was getting too crowded. Dad decided the time had come to kill off a few of the older birds and put them in the freezer.

We had never seen Dad attempt this before, but he said, "There is nothing to it."

He said that he would do this when he was a young man living on the farm. He knew we would all be involved in what he was about to do. He sat us all at the kitchen table to explain how and why this was necessary.

He asked us, "Do you like eating roast and fried Chicken?"

We all answered "Yes,"

"Do you like eating eggs?"

Again, we all answered "Yes."

"Would you like to live in this house with around twenty more kids, sharing your food, beds, and toys?"

"No" was our answer.

He tried to make the explanation as simple as possible.

He told us, "The older chickens no longer lay eggs, but they still eat as much food. To make room for the younger chicks to grow and to continue laying eggs, the older chickens must be sacrificed, and this will put food in the freezer. It may be harsh to watch, but remember, this is where the chicken on the table comes from. The chicken does not feel it; it happens too fast."

It was then time to do it. We all followed him to the coop, where he grabbed one of the older chickens. He walked to the driveway near the car, and he told us to "stay back on the grass."

He had placed a large railroad tie on the ground. Holding the chicken's neck in his left hand and laying it across the board, while in his right hand, he was wielding a small axe. With one swift swing of the axe, he chopped off the head. The chicken's head flew one way, while Dad tossed the body away from him. It was so weird to watch, the chicken without a head looked alive, as it jumped, and flopped all around the driveway. It took anywhere from ten to fifteen minutes for the chickens to die.

To me, this was disgusting and hard to watch. Dad would do anywhere from five to ten chickens at a time. Now, it was Mom's turn to take over. While Dad was killing the chickens, Mom had placed two large pots of water on the stove to boil. Dad would bring the dead chickens up to the porch for Mom. There, she would dip each chicken into the boiling water. She made sure that none of the kids got too close to the hot water.

After a while, she would take a chicken out of the pot and hand one to each of us. She had us sit on the edge of the porch and pluck the feathers from the bodies of the chickens. This job was not easy; the feathers were so hard to pull out to start with, and all the wet feathers would stick to your fingers. That was not the worst of it; wet chicken feathers stank so bad that I thought I would get sick.

After all the feathers were removed, Mom would take the chickens into the kitchen. She would place one at a time into the sink, taking a knife, she would cut a hole in the butt. She then would reach in and pull out all the insides, which included the heart, liver, and all of the other organs. She would pull everything out before washing the inside a few more times.

Once all the organs were out and the neck was cut off, she would be sure to wash everything thoroughly. After a few rinses, the chickens are all cleaned. It was time to wrap them and place them in the freezer. By this time, Dad was done outside and came in to help Mom get all the chickens ready for the freezer. The neck and all of the organs were placed back into the belly of each chicken. Dad would get the freezer paper out to wrap each chicken.

This process would take almost a full day. I would always be glad when the work was all done. Knowing we had food in the freezer made all the work worthwhile. I learned an important lesson that day, seeing what it took to put food on the table. Mom and Dad were so pleased with the way we all handled the stressful day of seeing chickens being killed that they asked us, "How would we like to go to a drive-in movie on Saturday?"

The only way to see a good movie in the late 1950s was to go to a movie theater.

Drive-In Movies

Disney was just starting to come out with children's movies, like "The Shaggy Dog," "Flobber," "Treasure Island," "Old Yeller," "Davy Crockett," and many more. These movies could not be seen on TV, and there were no DVDs or Cassettes. The shows we would watch on TV were western, like "Bonanza," "Gun Smoke," "Wagon Train," and "The Lone Ranger." "American Bandstand" was always one of our favorites.

The evening arrived for us to go to the drive-in.

Mom asked Dad, "Bring a newspaper home on your way back from the store."

They would then decide on what movie we would go to see. Mom had the younger boys take a nap, since it would be a late night out. Dad arrived home with the newspaper and sat at the table to decide where we would go. There were two drive-in theaters within driving distance of where we lived. Both were approximately one-half hour away.

One was in the community of Sinking Spring, and the other one was in the village of Temple, called the Reading Drive-in. I can't be sure what movie mom and dad selected that night, but we went to the Reading Drive-in.

Mom would get the boys dressed and pack a few peanut butter and jelly sandwiches. Dad would make a cooler full of fruit punch. Going to a drive-in with eight kids came with some problems.

Where would everyone sit to watch the movie? Surely not all in the car. Mom would take a chamber pot and two large blankets with her. The pot was for the small boys in case they had to pee or do whatever. The two large Blankets, we would lie them on the ground in front of the car. We had to be sure to place it within the sound coming from the speaker on a pole beside each car.

Dad would park as close to the concessions stand as possible. This made it easier for Nelson, Susie, and me, and the three older boys, to use the restrooms.

In the late 1950s, the Reading drive-in had a small electric train in front of the movie screen that we could ride. There were a few swings sets outside the concession stand. Before the movie started, this area was well lit, but when the movie started, all the lights went out. It would come across the loudspeaker and show on the screen the minutes and seconds left before the lights went off.

The foster boys on a swing set

We all arrived back at the car seconds before the lights were turned off. Finding the car in the dark would have been difficult, and boy! Did it get dark?

Back at the car, a few of the boys went into the car to watch the movie, while the rest of us sat on the blankets. At times, it was hard to hear what they were saying on the screen, but we seemed to manage. During the intermission, Mom would hand out the sandwiches and punch to those who wanted them. Susie and I just wanted to go down to the playground and go on the swings.

Again, it came across the loudspeaker when the second movie was to start, and again, we ran back to the car. I remember staying up late, playing at a playground, and watching a Disney movie was the highlight of my weekend.

One Day, our Aunt Shirley (Uncle Tom's Wife) came to our house and asked Mom, "How would the girls and a few of the boys like to go to town and see a movie?"

Mom said, "Well, let's ask them."

Mom called us into the living room and said, "Aunt Shirley is going to see a movie in town, and wants to know if you would like to go with?"

Since the weather was a little cool and we were only watching TV, we agreed.

Shirley said, "I will be ready in a few minutes, so go get your things."

About fifteen minutes later, Shirley returned to the house to pick us up. There were 5 of us going with her, Susie and I, plus two of the older boys and Nelson.

As we drove away, we asked Shirley, "What movies were playing?"

She said," There were a few playing that we may like to see."

There was one called "No Time for Sergeant," which was a comedy, and an Elvis movie titled "King Creole."

She then asked us which one we wanted to see. I was not into Elvis at the age of nine, so I went with Nelson and the two other boys to see "No Time for Sergeants." Susie wanted to see Elvis with Aunt Shirley. The theaters were right across the street from each other. Since both movies left around the same time, we agreed to meet in front of the theater that Susie and Aunt Shirley attended. The movie was great, and I was having a fun day.

Who knew how bad, life for me was going to get? We met Shirley and Susie as planned and headed back to the car. As we crossed over Sixth Street, right on the corner, was Woolworth, a five-and-ten-cent department store. Shirley wanted to get something in the store, since we were in town anyway.

As we entered the store, Shirley walked off looking for the items she wanted. The rest of us started looking around to see what we could find. I remember wandering around the store and how we all ended up close to the back. I could see Susie and the rest just looking around.

Only a few minutes had passed when I raised my head to see why I could no longer hear anyone talking. I remember turning around in a circle, yelling, "Susie, where are you?"

But no one answered. The longer I walked up and down the aisles, yelling, the more scared and stressed I was getting. Arriving at the front of the store, I was in tears. Being only nine years old and unfamiliar with the surroundings, fear was starting to overwhelm me.

A few people saw me crying and asked if I was all right. I was not sure what to say, since I did not know what was happening myself. I remember standing there for what felt like hours, but it was only a few minutes. It took a while before Shirley realized I was not with them and finally came back looking for me.

They found me crying while standing at the entrance to the store. I was so glad to see them. I could also see how stressed Shirley was, just knowing that she lost one of Mom's girls in the big city of Reading.

She asked me, "What happened, and why was I not with the rest of the kids?"

I told her, "I was just looking around, and then just like that, everyone was gone."

She told me that the car was just parked in the back of the store, so it did not take long for them to miss me. In a way, I was upset that no one knew I had not been with them for so long, but I did not say anything. I was so glad I was safe again and back with my family. It was not until many years later that I realized how much this incident affected me throughout the rest of my life.

To this day, I have a phobia of being some place, and being abandoned, and lost to the people I am with, and in a place I do not know. I come to believe that since I never thought much about this event, I must have convinced myself that it was another life lesson.

As Susie and I got older, simple things, like swimming, playing ball, and going to the playground, were not enough to keep us occupied; Mom saw we needed more.

She introduced us to Roller skating. This is something she did for a short time as a child. She never went to a rink, but would skate on the pavement in front of Nana's House.

Nana and John

Roller Skating

One day, when we were around ten years old, Mom took us to the Reading Fair Ground Skating Rink. We sat there for a while just watching the other skaters.

Mom asked us, "Would you like to give it a try?"

I do not know about Susie, but I recalled not being sure if this was something I wanted to do. It did look like a lot of fun, so why not give it a chance?

I overheard kids at school saying how much fun they had roller skating. Mom left for a little while and then returned with a pair of skates for each of us. Tell the truth, I was somewhat scared.

As soon as I stood up, I fell.

Mom said, "Come on, you can do it."

It did not take long for Susie and me to start skating around the rink. We would still fall, but with each trip around, we were getting better. It took a few more times at the rink before we were skating like we were doing it for a long time.

Mom asked us one day, "Do you guys want to take lessons?"

This would mean Mom would have to pay someone to teach us the fundamentals of figure skating. Not knowing what was involved in taking lessons, we agreed. I remember Mom buying each of us a cute full-piece blue skating outfit. They were beautiful, just like a professionals would wear. I am not sure how long we kept taking the lessons.

In later years, the race track and the whole Reading Fairgrounds were raised. Everything was removed, and the grounds were turned into a shopping mall. Mom found a different place to take up skating. She found the Sinking Spring rink. We would go there quite often, mainly on weekends. Going skating when I was still young was a great part of my youth, but I had no idea what a much bigger part it would play in my adult life. Before the Reading Fair turned into a shopping mall. This was the place to go every September.

The Reading Fair

The Reading Fair was one of the biggest fairs in the area. Schools would give out passes to all the students, and the schools would be closed on certain days. Besides having the stock car race track at the fairgrounds, there were many concession stands and rides. The midway would get packed with people every day the fair was open.

Mom and Dad took us to the fair at least twice. One warm day in September, traveling to the Reading Fair did not turn out as planned. All the kids had been at the fair a few times, and now it was Mom and Dad's turn to go on their own. They were going to see a girlie show. It was an evening that I will never forget. It was a warm late night around five pm, and the sun was lying low in the sky. We were all in the car and on our way to our Aunt Anna so she could babysit us. We were still too young to be left alone.

Nelson was the only one who stayed home alone since he was older. In a way, he was the lucky one, not having to deal with the tragedy that was about to unfold. This evening would become one of the darkest days in my life. Susie and I were sitting on the bench that sat behind the front seat and straddled the hump on the floor.

There were four boys in the back seat and two on Mom's lap in the front seat. We had only been on the road for about ten minutes. We were just coming down into Shillington to Lancaster Avenue, stopping at the red light at the bottom of the hill.

As soon as the light turned green, Dad continued straight ahead over Lancaster Avenue. We were going down the road approaching a 4 way stop sign intersection. Dad stopped the car and looked both ways before entering the intersection. He stepped on the gas and started to pull out, when out of nowhere, a large city bus ran a stop sign and hit our car broadside.

I remember seeing a large object approaching us out of the corner of my eye. It all happened so fast that I did not have time to say anything. It hit directly at Mom's door as Dad turned away from the bus to avoid the collision. The impact was so intense that it forced the bus onto a lawn and hit a house. The lady living in the house said that she thought her water heater blew up.

Mom's door was ripped off, and she and the two boys that she had on her lap were thrown out of the car and onto the sidewalk. Mom had the strength to hang on to the boys. When the ambulance arrived, they said that both boys were still in their mom's arms.

Dad was still in the car; he was thrown across the front seat and knocked out for a few minutes. Susie and I were not hurt, but both of us were thrown up over the front seat. The other four boys were also ok. I remember right after the collision, seeing mom lying on the curb, I forgot that the car we were in had four doors.

Lying on my stomach across the back of the front seat, I remember reaching across Dad to open the front door, as he lay on the seat. He was just coming to when I asked him if he was ok.

He said "Yes."

I could see that he did have a cut on his forehead, and the blood was running down his face. I remember looking over at Susie to be sure she was okay. She, too, was lying across the back of the front seat. I was so shaken up that I still tried to open the front door.

In a few seconds, I got my wits back, and I remembered the door right next to me. I opened it and ran over to Mom. I remember looking back at the car, and what I saw will stick in my mind forever. The side of the car where Mom was sitting was all smashed in, and her door was torn off. I could see how much pain she was in, but even with all she has been through, she said to me, "I am alright."

She then asked, "Is Dad and the other kids ok?"

I reassured her that everyone was ok and that she was the only one hurt. I could see the dirt and gravel embedded in her arms. Her shoes were missing, and her dress was torn and dirty. There were a few cuts that were bleeding profusely. The two boys were gently taken out of her arms and checked for any injuries by some bystanders.

Mom was told to stay seated until the ambulance arrived. I do not believe she could get up even if she wanted to. The ambulance was just pulling up and parked along the curb where Mom was sitting. A few other cars stopped to assist all the kids. They had us all sit on the curb and wait for the medical workers to check us out. We were all loaded into two ambulances and rushed to the hospital.

Mom was in bad shape, both of her arms were severely bruised, and she had some minor cuts and bruises over the rest of her body. She was only in the hospital for one day. When she came home, both arms were so swollen, and she was told that ice had to be applied to both arms a few times a day. As soon as the swelling went down, Dad had to take her to the hospital to have them re-x-rayed. The doctors reconfirmed that there were no broken bones.

The swelling in both arms has gone down, and the doctors told her she needed to start using them as much as possible. This was a hard time for Dad because not only did he go to work, but he had to do most of the housework and take care of all of us. Dad was a trooper and did a great job. Sure, one of our aunts came in to help, but it was still a hard time for all of us.

Once the swelling was completely gone, Mom, for a long time afterwards, would get a lot of pain in both arms. She never complained much, but at times we could see the pain in her eyes. It took a few more months until Mom was back to normal. This was another example of how far her love would go for the kids who lived in "The Hen House."

How many people could have hung on to the boys and kept them safe? I always knew Mom was a strong woman; this confirmed my belief in the love she had for her family.

This was one time in my life that I would rather forget, knowing I most likely will remember it forever. Remembering the happier times would bring closure to that terrible day.

Happier Occasions

Halloween

Looking back at some happier occasions, one time Susie and I spent on Halloween. Now that we were a little older, Mom had a great time dressing us all up to go trick or treating.

The outfit that I had was that of a kind. It was a full cotton body suit that I had to step into and tie at the neck. The mask was a hood that fell over my head and covered my whole face. It had long floppy ears, and it was so cute. There were still not that many houses around us on the mountain. Mom left us to roam down the hill to Mohnton. This was a much larger community.

Mom would save all of her large shopping bags, just for us, so we had something to put our candy in. These bags were the largest shopping bags you could get; each had two handles. We would leave the house right before it got dark. We only had one flashlight to share. We were never scared of roaming around late at night; we saw this as one of many adventures.

Starting at the top of the mountain and working our way down the hill, we would hit every house along the way. Most people were very nice and gave us money instead of candy, like half dollars and quarters. We did come across a few houses that just slammed the door in our faces. There was one house where a man slammed the door in our faces, used a few nasty words, and told us to get lost.

We never took it personally when someone did not open the door or give us anything, but this took it too far. We knew we wanted to do something to him for being so rude, but what? We searched the ground for something to use to teach him a lesson.

Lying on the ground around some garbage cans were some small toothpicks. I picked up the toothpicks, not knowing how we could use them. Standing around thinking, was there anything else we could use?

I was still holding the toothpicks when someone suggested that we stick the toothpicks in the side of the doorbell and break them off. We were not sure if this was going to work or not, but we did it. After breaking off the toothpicks, his doorbell would not stop ringing.

As we were coming up the opposite side of the road, he was still on the porch trying to dig out the toothpicks. He glanced at us and gave us a dirty look, but we could not stop laughing. We would stay out for a few hours and then start the long hike back up the mountain.

Arriving home, Mom would check out all of our bags. She said, "There are some sick people in the world, and checking our candy was for our safety."

Once she was satisfied everything was ok, she left us to take the bags to our rooms. Mom and Dad were surprised at how much candy we each had. Each of our bags was at least half full. We would do this at least twice. We all had enough candy to share with the smaller boys. No one went without. Mom liked Halloween as much as we did.

The Cedar Top Fire Company was having a Halloween party on Saturday. Mom and Aunt Shirley, who lived right down the road from us, decided to design their costumes. There was going to be food and a costume contest.

Mom and Shirley got two large cardboard boxes and painted them both white. They then put black dots on each to make a pair of dice and then attached straps that go over their shoulders so they could hold them up.

I will never forget the way they looked walking down the road to the fire company. Their costumes were so different from anything at the party. Of course, they won a prize. Sure, more candy, just what we needed. It was a fun evening; we all ate and laughed.

Happy occasions were always waiting to happen.

Best Christmas Ever

I do not think that anyone could have had a better Christmas.

Susie and I were around ten or eleven years old. I am not sure
of the year. The house was full of kids. Mom and Dad started
getting ready for Christmas months in advance. They had plenty of
work to do. This was the year they went over the top with gifts. For
days, something was going on in secret, but what?

I would find out years later how hard it was for Mom and Dad
to hide for weeks, the big surprise they were planning. Every night
after supper and late into the night, Dad would disappear.

Getting everything ready took up a lot of his time. Before his
secret disappearing act, there was the tree and all of the decorations
to put up. Dad loved setting up the tree. He would go buy a large
eight-foot piece of plywood and place it on two saw horses.

A few years before, Nelson had gotten a Lionel train set for
Christmas. Dad had been collecting Plasticville Houses for years to
place under the tree. Each year, he added one or two more
buildings. He, too, collected all the accessories to make a beautiful
country Christmas village. He had the train, a train tunnel, all of
the track to go around the full span of the large wooden platform,

trees, street lights, people, a piece of oval glass for a pond, stop signs, cars, and stop lights.

He stared down at all the cardboard boxes and was like a child in a candy shop, trying to figure out which one to start with. It was now time to go for a tree. He wanted a tree large enough to hit the ceiling. It needed to be at least five feet tall. He would take two or three kids with him to fetch a tree.

The sun was setting, but he said that he still had time to get a tree. He would take an axe with him to cut it down. At a tree farm, trees were fairly cheap, only a few dollars, but the only thing was that you had to cut them down yourself.

We arrived at the tree farm and started to walk around. The trees were scattered all around the large field. The price depended on the size of the tree and what type it was. We each walked around and picked out a tree we liked. Dad would check out each tree, and considering the shape and the price, he decided on the tree we would take home.

Dad could not afford one of the better trees, but we did manage to find a beautiful one at a reasonable price. Dad tied the tree to the top of the car for the ride home.

Arriving home, he could see the kids watching out of the picture window to get a glimpse of the tree. Mom was waiting at the open door as he carried the tree in. He already had the metal tree stand on top of the platform. As he lifted the tree, the top hit the ceiling, but with a quick move, the trunk fell into the stand.

Mom held it as Dad tightened the screws around the stem that would hold the tree in place.

Mom asked Dad, "Is it possible to cut a bit off the top so the angel would fit?"

"Oh yes," he said, "I forgot about the angel."

Mom handed him a small saw, and he took a few inches off the top. Now that the tree was standing straight, it was time for the lights. Dad got a large box out that had a few strings of lights in it. He sat on one chair while Mom sat on another to untangle each string of lights.

He plugged each set in to be sure each light came on. If he found any bulb that did not light, he would replace it with a new one. The lights were ready to be placed on the tree. Dad had to stand on the platform to get the lights around the back of the tree.

As he stood on the platform, his mom handed him the angel.

He placed her on the top of the tree and said, "How does she look?"

Mom said, "She is perfect."

It only took him around twenty minutes to get the few strings of lights wrapped around the tree. It was now time to plug them in, and we all stood back while Dad placed the end of the cord into the wall socket.

Dad looked over us and asked, "Are you ready?"

As he placed the plug in, and the lights came on, we just stood there and took in the beauty of all the different colored lights. Dad was tired by this time, and he had to go to work the next day. It was also time for all the kids to go to bed.

He said that he would finish decorating the tree tomorrow after work. Susie and I were so excited about Christmas. The wait was excruciating, but what else could we do?

The following evening, supper was earlier than normal, and Susie and I had to help Mom clean up the supper dishes. We wanted more than anything to be in the living room with Dad, but we knew there would be plenty of time to watch Dad finish the tree.

Once we were done cleaning up, we headed into the living room. Dad pulled another large box out from under the platform. He lifted off the top to expose hundreds of glass Christmas balls and ornaments. Dad stood on the platform again to hang a few ornaments around the far sides of the tree. The platform with the village lay right in front of a living room picture window, but where the tree stood, it was more in the corner of the living room.

The back of the tree faced a wall, so there was no need to place ornaments back there. Dad finished putting the ornaments and got down off the platform. We were sitting, waiting for our chance to help decorate the tree.

Dad opened another large box of ornaments and said, "Pick out two each."

We took turns picking out the ornaments we wanted to hang on the tree. One at a time, we approached the tree and hung the ornaments. Dad lifted the smaller boys so they could reach up high enough. The tree was almost done; all it needed was some silver tinsel. Mom came into the living room with a few boxes of tinsel. She sat on the sofa and opened one box at a time. She handed each of us a few strands.

We took the tinsel back to Dad, he said, "Take a strand or two and throw it on the tree."

The tree was all decorated and ready to see what it looked like with the lights on. Dad switched off the living room table lights. He again plugged the tree in, and I could see the beautiful lights twinkling in his eyes. I could see on his face how pleased he was with the tree.

Mom was still sitting on the sofa when I noticed her black hair was changing colors from the reflection coming from the lights. Dad was halfway done. He now had the village to assemble. Mom had bought some brick-printed paper to put around the front and side of the platform. Dad stored all of the empty boxes under the platform. This would hide the boxes that held all the decorations until it was time to take the tree down.

Viewing the tree from the kitchen, it lit up the entire living room. The lights flickered on and off like a beating heart, and the ceiling had a geometric design. The living room was transformed into a place of beauty and wonder.

Either Dad or Nelson would sit at the train transformer. They left each boy take a turn running the train. Dad had some liquid in a small bottle. He would place a few drops in the smoke stack of the train. As the train went around the track, smoke could be seen puffing out into the air.

While Nelson showed the boys how to run the train, Dad opened a large bag of white cotton and placed it all over the platform, duplicating the snow for his village. It was time to add all of the houses. Each house had to be put together before placing it on the platform.

There were houses, stores, churches, schools, depots, and factories. He would place the trees, light poles, and a piece of glass for an ice-skating pond, with all the ice skaters, a park, and the stop lights.

Next came all of the people. The people were positioned to give the village an authentic look. Positioned behind the tree, Dad placed a large tunnel over the train track. The tree was now all ready for Santa. There were still a little over two more weeks before Christmas.

At this time, Dad started to disappear for a few hours every evening. I found the door to Mom and Dad's bedroom was always locked. I got a peek into the room one evening when Mom opened it to go in. I saw a large blanket covering something in the far end. The bedroom was not that big, so whatever it was, it took up a large part of it.

You can imagine my curiosity and the suspense of not knowing what was under the blanket. I ran upstairs to tell Susie what I saw. With all that's happening, we felt that, on Christmas morning, we would understand the mystery.

It was finally time for Christmas vacation to start. Only three more days it would be Christmas, and the suspense would be over.

Christmas Eve was full of wonder and love.

Mom and Dad sat with all of us playing with the train and watching Christmas movies on the TV. This was one night when we did not hesitate when it was time to go to bed. We all knew the sooner we went to sleep, the sooner Santa would be here.

Susie and I were old enough not to believe in Santa, but believing for one more night was so much fun. It had to be after midnight when we heard something moving around in the living room. Since we no longer believed in Santa, we knew it had to be Mom and Dad. I do not know what time it was when I finally fell asleep, but before I knew it, the sun had come up. Before we could get out of bed, someone knocked on our door.

Someone said, "Come on, it's time to see what Santa left."

As we approached the living room, my eyes opened so wide that I thought they would fall out of my head. There were at least five full-size bicycles, three boys and two girls, two new American Flyer sleds, two tricycles, two red wagons, and so many wrapped packages that it was hard to see the furniture. Now, we knew what Dad was doing every evening.

Putting together each bike would take a few hours. Susie and I knew the two blue Schwinn girl bikes were for us. If the bikes were the only item we got, I would have been overjoyed, but there was so much more. The older boys also got a bike, and the smaller boys each got wagons and tricycles.

Sitting on each chair and the sofa were piles of wrapped

presents with a name on them. Each of us got a pile to unwrap.

There was so much paper flying that you could not see the floor. Mom and Dad would spend all their extra money to ensure we had a wonderful Christmas. I can honestly say that I never saw Mom and Dad exchange gifts. They may have done it in secret, but I will never know. We had the best Christmas ever.

After cleaning up all of the paper, we were told to take our presents to our rooms. It was still early morning when Mom said, "It's time for breakfast."

I could not take my eyes off my new bike. The weather was still too cold to take them outside, but just knowing the day would come was enough. The bikes sat in the living room for a few days. I would sit on it to watch TV every evening.

It was time to put the bikes, wagons, and sleighs in the basement. Dad and Nelson took them all down the steps. The basement had a cement floor and was not very large.

Mom said, "If we were careful, we could ride our bikes in a circle."

Foster boys in the basement with their new Christmas toys

First, Susie and I had to clean up the dishes; this was one of our everyday chores. The boys would do the laundry and get the smaller boys dressed.

Once our chores were done, we could go to our rooms to play with whatever toy we got, or into the living room to watch TV.

Now that everything had settled down, it was time for Mom to start the large Christmas dinner. She would make a large Turkey and all of the fixings. Dad peeled the potatoes while Mom prepared the turkey for the oven.

In a few hours, there would be one of the best Christmas dinners anyone could pray for. Mom was a great cook. On Christmas Eve, Mom had made one of her famous Chocolate Pies. She made it with pure cocoa and a lot of love. Dad set the table and poured everyone a glass of water. It was time to eat. Dad called us all to come to the table. The smell of all the food filled the house with an aroma that had your mouth watering.

As soon as everyone had been seated, Dad started serving the food. He served turkey, potatoes, and whatever vegetables we wanted on each plate. No one was forced to eat anything they did not care for, after all, it was Christmas.

It was Susie and my job to clean up the kitchen. We did not mind, and it did not take us that long. I would wash, and Susie would dry. We put all the dishes away, wiped off the table, and swept the floor. Dad and one of the older boys would help Dad scrape the dishes and place them into the sink. When all the work was done, it was time to sit back, relax, and digest our food.

Sitting on the sofa, my eyes kept going to my new bike. I never thought that I would get such a wonderful gift.

Growing up in the house I called "The Hen House" was wonderful and taught me an invaluable lesson.

Life is not always what we may have wanted or expected, but if you accept what life has thrown your way, you will turn into a loving and caring person, just like my Mom and Dad.

A Lifestyle Change

Going from a little girl to a young lady came early for Susie and me one cold day in early spring. We just turned 12 years old in January and were looking forward to spring and summer. We knew our bodies were changing, and we were not those little girls who wanted to play cowboys and Indians in the woods. We were now thinking of what clothes to wear, our hairstyle, and the boys.

I am not sure if Mom was ready for this big change. It all came to a head one day, and this is when Mom knew she could not ignore it any longer. Susie had to go to the bathroom as I waited for her. I heard her calling for me. I was wondering what she wanted.

As I opened the door, she said, "Close it."

I turned around, closed the door, and asked, "What's wrong?"

She was still sitting on the toilet when she said, "Come here."

In a way, I was scared. Why was she being so mysterious?

I walked a little bit closer when she said, "Look."

As I looked down, I was somewhat puzzled. There, in her

underwear, was a small spot of blood. She was so bewildered and was shaking a bit. As I stood there, not knowing what to do, I wondered what was happening to her.

She said, "You better go get Mom."

I said, "Okay,"

I opened the door and went to the living room. Mom and Dad were watching TV. I bent down to whisper in Mom's ear and asked her to follow me to the bathroom, where Susie was still sitting.

I locked the door behind us as Mom asked, "What's wrong?"

As she approached, Susie said, "Look." Susie then asked Mom, "What is it from?"

Mom said, "Don't worry, you are now a young lady."

I looked at Susie as she asked, "What does that mean?"

Not yet having sex education in school, we did not know what was happening.

Mom turned to me and told me that I needed to get on my bike and go down to Helen's. Helens was a small store, one and a half miles from our house.

I asked her, "What am I buying at the store?"

She said, "I will call, and what we need will be waiting for you."

She came out of the bathroom and gave me a few dollars. I still did not know what to think about the whole thing, but I did what Mom asked me to do. I jumped on my bike and headed to the store. I arrived at the store in a few minutes, and Helen was waiting for me.

She said, "Here are the things your mom asked for."

I paid for the bag of items and left the store. I placed the bag in my basket and I rushed to get back home. It only took me approximately twenty minutes to get to the store and back. Mom came out and asked me to follow her back into the bathroom. She wanted to explain what was going on and what else to expect. She gave a vague explanation and handed Susie one of the items in the bag.

As she showed Susie how to put on the belt, she asked me to open the box and give her one of the pads. Still not knowing what this was all for, I did what she asked. I watched everything Mom was showing Susie with great interest. Susie put on the belt & pad mom gave her, and we walked out of the bathroom. Only having one bathroom, one of the boys was waiting to use it.

She told us to sit at the kitchen table for a more detailed

explanation. We both sat down and listened to every word Mom was saying. Now that we knew that this was normal and happens to every young girl at some time, we understood how to handle it. I believe mom did not think this would happen to us at such an early age, and we would learn about this in school.

Well, that never happened; sex education classes were never offered to us while attending junior high school. I was then wondering when it was going to happen to me. I was so relieved that Susie was ok. I had it in the back of my mind that maybe I would never experience this and still become a young lady. Never needing any of the items in the bag. Well, that did not happen the way I planned. My nightmare began in the seventh grade, sitting in math class. Math class just ended, and my next class was physical education. I left the math class and headed for the gym. I arrived in the gym in a few minutes and opened my locker. I reached around my back and pulled down the zipper on my skirt.

As I slid down my skirt, one of my classmates said, "Sandy, what is all over your slip?"

I quickly turned it around, and I was so embarrassed. I could see that the entire back of my slip was covered in a bright red color. I knew just what it was, but why now? The gym teacher was quickly called over, and she told the rest of the students to go onto the gym floor. I was so upset, but she stayed there to help me clean up.

Since I had on a nylon slip, it absorbed all of the blood. The teacher asked me to take off my slip, and she helped me wash it out. Surprisingly, there was no blood on my skirt. She hung my slip up to dry. She headed for the office and came out with the items I needed, just like the ones in the bag Mom got for Susie.

She asked me, "Did I know how to put it on?"

I said, "Yes."

She told me, "I would be ok with just my skirt on until the slip dried."

I sat on the bleachers for the rest of the class watching the girls play basketball. I was surprised that no one said anything after leaving the gym. You know how gossip goes around a school in only minutes. Before getting on my bus at the end of the day, I went to the gym and picked up my slip. The gym teacher placed my slip into a plastic bag. She handed it to me as I entered the locker room and assured me I would be all right. I put it into my school bag.

I smiled all the way home, knowing I was a young lady and not a child any longer. I realized that becoming a young lady could not be this easy; life had more surprises for me to overcome.

Me sitting on a Sofa

Thirteenth Birthday Party

Now, Susie and I were going to be teenagers, and life would be different. Turning thirteen meant you were no longer a child, but somewhere between a child and an adult, and that came with some difficulties. There were times I wanted to act like a child, but on the other hand, I also wanted to be treated as an adult. Being stuck in between became a confusing time in my life. Mom could see occasions when we did not know how to act.

One day, Dad had to go for some milk and bread, and he asked Susie and me to go with him. We were in our bedroom listening to records and not doing anything special. Dad grabbed the 4 milk jugs and we followed him to the car.

There was a farm north of Reading where Dad would get glass gallon jugs of farm-fresh milk. We loved spending time with Dad as much as we did with Mom. He seemed to take the long way around and not to be in any hurry. We were gone for almost two hours. Arriving home, we did not notice anything different.

Dad opened the front door, and I asked, "Where are Mom and the kids?" It was so quiet.

He said, "I am not sure, why don't you both check out the

basement?"

I opened the door to the basement and did not see anything.

Susie yelled down the stairs, "Mom, are you down there?"

Still no answer. I could see the cellar light was lit. We both started down the steps, all of a sudden, everyone jumped out and yelled, "Happy Birthday!" Thank God I was holding on to the rail, or I may have fallen down the steps.

In the back of my mind, I felt something was up, but I was still so surprised. In the basement were a few of our friends from school, aunts and uncles, and some neighbors. Sitting on top of a long table was a beautiful birthday cake and two stacks of presents. Mom had brought our record player down from our room so we could play some music and dance. We celebrated like it was New Year's Eve, eating and dancing with our friends, and some older adults joined in. Watching them all dancing made the festivities more special.

After a while, it was time to eat. Mom had some cold food on the table: crackers, bologna, pretzels, chips, bread and more. We all sat around eating and talking. Now it was time to open our gifts. We opened each duplicate package together, so that one did not open something the other had not seen yet. I remember getting an orange and black flannel shirt.

As we held them up, I remarked, "Well, at least we won't get lost in a crowd."

We continued to open more of the gifts. There were more items, like a purse, a blouse, and a pair of pants, you get the picture. The last thing we opened was from Mom and Dad. It was something we both wanted. There were new pairs of ice skates. We already knew how to roller skate, so we wanted to know if ice skating was the same. The party lasted for a few hours, and the time came for everyone to leave. Susie and I were so happy waving goodbye to our neighbors and friends, knowing they took time out of their day to attend our birthday party, which was a special gift. Not everyone gets a thirteenth birthday party. This party was not only a celebration for the year we were born, but a transitional part of our lives.

When I looked back on what had taken place in my life over the last year, I was unsure if I wanted to be an adult. There was so much more to growing up than I ever bargained for.

Funny Times at the Hen House

Living in the Hen House came with some funny moments. Dad always wanted a Dog. As a child, he never had a real childhood or a dog. He had to work most of the time and had no time for a pet.

Mom heard him talking about it to some of the older boys. He would never get one without talking to Mom first, and he thought he knew what she would say. 'With the kids, the chicken coop, and working every day, you cannot have me take care of a dog.'

Boy, was he wrong! One day, he came home from work and was waiting on the front lawn where Mom and all of the kids were. As he got out of the car, he saw the most adorable Boxer dog he had ever seen. This was still a puppy, only a few months old, but Dad loved what he saw. He did not know how Mom knew what kind of dog he wanted, but as the old saying goes, she's a woman. Women know things that others do not know. This was an outside dog, but for a few months, he would stay in the basement.

Dad would bring him upstairs now and then to play with. It

did not take long for him to grow up to weigh around sixty pounds. He was a huge, muscular dog. Dad decided that keeping him in the basement was no longer a good idea. He had some extra lumber lying around the house, and started building a dog house so he could be tied outside.

This was a large house, and it weighed a lot. It took all that dad and some of the kids had to place it into the spot dad had picked out. In front of the house was a small yard that faced the driveway. This was a perfect spot for him. He could watch the comings and goings without getting bored.

Dad tied him out one day, and he seemed to like his house. He would go in and out of it all day long. I do not think he was so happy when night fell, but he did not make a sound. When Dad got up the next morning, he went to the large picture window on the front side of the house. When he looked out, he was surprised. There was no dog or even a dog house.

What happened? Where did he go? He quickly opened the front door and ran to find his dog and the house. As he made his way around the front of the house, he heard barking from under the window. As heavy as that dog house was, he managed to drag it up to the wall of the house, approximately twenty feet from where Dad had placed it.

When Dad came into the house, he had been laughing so hard

his face was turning red.

Mom asked him, "What is so funny?"

He said. "You will never guess what that silly dog did."

He told Mom everything, and she said, "You're kidding," and had to go out and see for herself. No one could believe that he was that strong. Dad and the boys had to put the house back in place, and this time, Dad anchored it down.

Dad said, "I want to see him pull it around the yard now."

Dad was on his way home from work, and Mom was fixing supper around 4 o'clock on a rainy day in May. Susie and I were in the living room watching television when we heard the weirdest noise. It sounds like someone was shooting a machine gun. The boys came running out of their rooms looking as confused as we were. Mom dropped what she was doing to help everyone look for the noise. She went from room to room and back to the kitchen. Dad pulled up in the driveway and came into the house.

No sooner than he asked "what was going on," he heard the same sound.

Mom looked at Dad and asked, "What is that?"

Dad said, "I do not know."

He spent a few minutes looking around and then decided to go

151

outside. Standing on the front lawn, he heard the same sound, but it was not as loud. He looked on the roof and there, it was, a beautiful colored woodpecker. He was pecking away on the TV antenna. When we were in the house, his tapping amplified the sound. A few minutes later, the woodpecker realized it was not making any progress and flew away. As the years rolled on, we all loved, laughed, and grew together.

Dad said that he was not a lucky man; if something could go wrong, it did. One mid-fall day, the leaves were falling, the sun set early in the sky, and Dad had come home with his new used car. A brand-new car was never in the budget. He parked it in the driveway, and we all ran out to look it over. He was so proud of his purchase.

A few months went by, and the car was running perfectly. One day, he went to the store for Mom. The items she needed could not be bought at Helen's, the local country store. It was no easy living on top of a mountain; no matter which road you took, it led you down a steep hill. There were four different roads, two to Mohnton, one to Kenhorst, and one to Shillington. Dad decided to take the one that led to Shillington. This was a very steep and winding road. He finished at the store and headed for home.

Going down the steep hill went as normal, but it was going back up that Dad realized he had a problem. As he approached the incline, the car did not want to go. It just sat at one spot at the bottom of the hill with the engine running. Dad was somewhat puzzled. He tried a few times, but the car would not go up the hill. He decided to turn the car around and head back down the hill.

While backing the car up to turn around, he realized it would go up the hill backwards. He started to move slowly to see just what would happen. He could not believe it would go up in reverse but not forward. He managed to get to the top of the hill and turn around. Now that he was on mostly level roads with only small hills, the car seemed to work just fine once more. I do not remember if Dad ever had the car fixed.

My Dad's car

Junior High

Eighth and ninth grade were two years of turmoil for Susie and me. Neither of us was very smart, or learned very fast to hate school. We were not very popular and had few friends. I do not know if we were singled out because we did not conform to what a teenager should look like. I believe it was the way we dressed.

Fashion had a significant impact on the way a person was treated. Self-describing, I could see myself looking like a bag lady at age seven. I had no figure and was flat as a pancake. there was nothing, no hips, no breasts, no rear end, very long skinny legs, and no pretty facial features. We both wore glasses, and our hair was so thin and fine that no matter what we did with it, it would not hold a curl.

I am not sure what era in time would have suited me better, maybe the roaring twenties, I could have been a Flapper. In this era, hats were worn, breasts were smaller, and long, thin legs were the style. Maybe the forties would have simplified my life with even bigger hats and longer dresses. Our clothes were always clean and showed no wear, but they never made a fashion statement.

Growing up in the late fifties and early sixties came with some challenges. The early sixties came with short dresses, which only helped to point out my long, thin legs, and small crop tops that only drew attention to my small breasts.

In the early sixties, all females had to wear a dress or skirt to school. The fashion was to wear the skirt or dress very short, above the knees. Mom, I must admit, was a little old-fashioned and only bought us skirts that came below our knees. To make things worse, Susie and I only had a few outfits to wear to school. I can remember having two wool skirts, a gray one and a blue one. There was a brown jumper and a blouse to go under it. We only had two or three colored blouses, one pair of dress shoes, and a pair of sneakers. Wearing the same items day after day did not help with my fashion image.

After arriving at school, Susie and I wanted to look like the other girls, we went right to the ladies' room where we could roll up our skirts at the waist. This did not always look too good. Everyone could see the gathering around the waist.

Even though Susie and I did not have much, it was strange; we never complained. I do not remember ever asking for any new clothes. Now and then, Mom would buy something for us. She could tell when doing the laundry if something new was needed. We tried to mix things up, to make it look like we had more outfits than we did. You would think that since mom and dad had all of the foster boys to buy for, we would have felt left out, but we never had any feelings one way or the other. Mom would get vouchers from the foster care system to buy clothes for the boys.

Susie and I learned to deal with being bullied and tried our best to make friends. Being bullied day after day took its toll on both of us. We were called four eyes, the hen twins, scab, and many more names. I tried my best to get along with everyone, but every school has its cliques.

This is where the popular kids hang out together and the unpopular kids go their way. We did have a good friend by the name of Shirley, who was in the popular clique but treated us as friends. She treated Susie and me as equals and did not call us names. Since we did not have many friends, having a twin helped with the torment. We always knew that at least we would have each other to lean on.

Shirley was also a close neighbor, living right up the lane from our house. We would go to her house and put on plays in her basement, listen to records, and do homework together. While at school, she would hang out with the popular clique, but she was never mean to us. Susie and I tried our best to get good grades, but not being liked had a negative effect. I would read and study, but nothing seemed to stick in my mind. I would forget everything the moment I enter the school building the following day.

Every day at school, there was an activity that I looked

forward to. Each of the two lunch periods would last approximately thirty-five minutes. Half of the students would have the first lunch period, while the second half would go to the gym to listen to records and dance on the gym floor. I loved to dance and felt so free from everything and everyone around me. I could just let go and close my eyes to the bullying I knew would again happen once I returned to class, but at least for a few minutes, I was in a different world.

Why Susie and I continued to pass was a mystery; it seemed like the school system was failing us by pushing us from one grade to the next without earning it.

There was one time in the ninth grade that I thought my luck was turning. I would see girls wearing a ring around their neck on a chain. I know this meant they were going steady with a boy. He may or may not attend our school. There was a rumor that a new boy was coming to school in a few days. He was a friend of one of the popular students.

One day, I saw him walk into one of my classes. I watched him stroll past me and take a desk in the back of the room. At this age, I thought he was so cute. I am not sure of his name anymore, but for some reason, the name Joe keeps coming to mind.

During idol conversation, I told a few close friends how cute I thought he was. Somehow it got back to him, and he asked me for a date the following Friday. I was beside myself. Could this be happening?

He said "right after school, he would walk be the road to the shopping center in Shillington."

I had told Mom and Dad that I may need a ride home after my date, and they were ok with it.

Mom said, "Just call, and Dad will come for you."

Mom knew of our problems in school and felt this was an encouraging sign. Friday was here, and school was letting out. I said goodbye to Susie and met Joe waiting outside the front door. He gently took my hand and smiled. Walking to the drug store, I had butterflies in my stomach.

My first date ever, and things were going so well. We entered the drug store and sat at one of the booths. Not knowing what to talk about, we just sat there for a few minutes. The waitress came over and he ordered two chocolate sodas. I felt like I was in heaven. We finally started to talk to each other about family and school.

According to our conversation, I had a feeling he liked me. We were there for around 2 hours. I was enjoying myself and did not realize how late it was getting. It was time to call Dad. We finished our soda, and Joe walked me out of the store to use the phone. Dad was there in 15 minutes.

I said, "goodbye," and he kissed me on my cheek.

As soon as I arrived home, Susie was waiting for me and asked me how it went. I told her it was great. So, this is what it is like to be in love. I know now that I had no idea what love was all about, but at the time, I was in love. I had to wait a whole weekend before I would see him again.

This was the first time I wanted the weekend to be over, so I could go back to school. How could I know that my world was about to come crashing down? Susie and I went to Shirley's house on Saturday to listen to some records. I could see in her eyes that something was wrong.

I said, "Shirley, I know there is something on your mind. Would you like to talk about it?" She said, "I hate to tell you, but the date you had was just a ruse."

The popular kids found out how much you liked Joe and wanted to see how far you would go with him."

I asked, "What do you mean?"

She said, "he was going to be nice to you for a week and then ask you to go to the football game with him next weekend. The popular kids had a bet that Joe would take advantage of you under the bleachers, and you would not resist."

I was devastated and started to cry. Is this all I was, a game to some selfish kids? Do my feelings mean nothing to them? I cried for a while and told her I was so grateful to her for letting me know.

I told her, "I learned a lesson, boys can be cruel and their attentions are not always what they seem, I will never let a boy take advantage of me, I am now too smart for that."

I told her not to worry about me, and that I would see Joe on Monday and let him know what I think of him. As I entered the school building, he walked up to me, and I just gave him a look of disgust.

As some of the popular students stood in the background to see what was about to happen next, he asked me, "What's wrong?"

I said, "You tell me."

By the look on my face, Joe said, "You know, don't you?"

I said, "I know the whole story, how could you?"

With no feelings or shame, He said, "Well, I least I tried."

As much as I hated him at this point, I just turned and walked away. I could feel the tears streaming down my cheeks, but I was not going to show him how I felt. I wanted to run away to be alone, but the school bell was ringing. I left the area and walked to class. This would wait until I got home. Life had thrown me some foul balls, but I have become a stronger person despite them.

When Mom heard what happened with Joe, she and Dad were upset. If Dad had seen Joe, he might have punched him out. Dad was a gentle man, but ruffle his feathers, and he could become a lion.

Mom tried to help ease my disappointment by letting Susie and me go roller skating, where she knew there would be boys our age who did not attend our school. The Sinking Spring roller ring was in the community of Sinking Spring, about eight miles from where we lived. I must say the freedom of skating and not thinking about what had happened was just what I needed.

It took a few days back at school for me to forget that day, which mentally could have destroyed the rest of my life. Mom and Dad were pleased to see that I was no longer upset, and I seemed to get my life back to normal. I knew that this was an experience that I would never forget completely. I was not going to let it affect any future relationships with boys.

Skating was a pleasure, since no one knew who we were. Boys would ask us to slow dance. Holding hands and skating around the outer ring while the organist played a slow song. Sinking Spring roller rink had an outer ring and an inner ring. The more experienced skaters would skate pretty fast on the outer ring, while the inner ring was for slower skaters and those learning to skate.

Mom knew that skating was not going to be enough. She knew we did not want to go skating every weekend. Susie and I would stay up in our bedroom and listen to records, and we loved to go dancing at a place called the Reck. This was a small hall down the hill on Lancaster Avenue in Shillington. It has just opened, and many of the kids from our school went there on a Friday night.

There was a small fee to get in, and a teacher to supervise and play the records. The teacher would also have bottles of soda for sale for ten cents each. As you walked in the front door, you would enter a wide-open room with benches running along each wall. The popular kids would sit on one side while the rest of us sat on the other.

The teacher would start the record player, and we would get up from where we were sitting. The popular kids were all paired off as boyfriends and girlfriends. The group we were with was all girls, and we had to dance with each other. Since we had no dates, we had to sit out all the slow dances.

As we all sat on the benches, we prayed for a boy to come and ask us to dance. Many boys came stag and would look around to see who was all there. We would anticipate maybe this would be the night a boy would ask us to dance, but it never happened.

Despite not being asked to dance, and since we love dancing, we still had a great time. Right up the road was a large church that held social dancing on a Saturday night. This was also down the hill, right off Lancaster Avenue. The dance was located in the basement of a church. There was also a minimum fee to get in, but it was well worth it. This was also a large room with chairs along the walls. Neither Susie nor I were ever asked to dance; by this time, we were used to it, and just made up our minds to have a good time, and not worry about the boys. We concluded that if it happened, it happened.

We learned a lot about ourselves in the process of skating and dancing. We found that the world would not end if a boy had never seen us as someone they would like to spend time with. While I was a child, I looked forward to being older, but no one told me that being an adult would come with so many heartbreaks and disappointments. I was at the stage when I had to decide what I wanted out of life.

The "Train of Life" was passing me by, and I had no idea where I would get off. I was never sure if Susie wanted the same things I did. I was so confused. What did I want?

Maybe doing better in school or leaving school and getting a job was the answer. I was only 14 years old and already had this on my mind. I decided to let life go on as it has been, and hope the answer will come to me over time. This is exactly what happened a few months later.

Turning the Corner

School was over for the summer, and the Tenth grade would not start until September. We were looking forward to the warm weather and not having to worry about the unfair treatments we received in school. It was like a breath of fresh air.

It was sometime in mid-July when a girlfriend of mom and her husband, and their two daughters, stopped in to see how mom and dad were doing.

They said that they were on their way to the Oley fair. The older daughter, Virginia, was also a foster child and was a bit older than we were. The other daughter, Darlene, was more our age.

As mom and her girlfriend sat in the living room talking, she suggested that maybe Susie and I would like to go with them to the fair and sleep over at their house. We were standing beside Mom when she was asked, hoping she would say yes. Mom looked at Dad, and they both agreed we could go.

Dad told Mom's girlfriend they would pick us up at their house sometime tomorrow afternoon. Susie and I ran to our rooms to get clothes and pack a bag for the night. Mom gave us each a few dollars to spend at the fair. We had never been to this fair before, but we were told that it had a lot of rides and food stands.

Arriving at the fair, we went our separate ways. Darlene and I went one way, while Susie and Virginia disappeared around one of the buildings. We had been walking around for some time, eating and going on a few rides. Arriving at the large Ferris wheel, we saw Susie and Virginia waiting in line. They sat in one seat, and Darlene and I stepped into the following seat.

We had circled a few times when we noticed two boys looking up at us. I yelled to Susie and Virginia, "Do you see the two boys down there?"

Susie yelled back, "Yes."

I tried to get their attention, and I started throwing a few of my hairpins. I eventually hit one of them. They looked up and waved, but to my disappointment, they waved at Susie and Virginia. The Ferris wheel was slowing up and letting off some riders. Susie and Virginia stepped off the Ferris Wheel and walked over to where the two boys were standing. The Ferris Wheel moved slightly, and it was our turn to get off. I wondered if the two boys would still be there.

As we got off, we did see them, but the tall one with the coal black hair and dark complexion started to talk to Virginia. Being looked over again was like just one more kick in the teeth. I watched from a distance and could not believe what I was seeing.

What is wrong with me? Why do boys look right past me? Am I invisible? As Susie departed the Ferris wheel, the shorter boy with blond hair started to talk to her. The boys introduced themselves as Donald and Rodney.

Darlene and I strolled in the background, watching Susie and Donald holding hands as they walked. Rodney was somewhat shy, so all they did was talk as they walked together. It was time to leave, and the boys walked Susie and Virginia to the car, with us following behind. Leaning against the car, they exchanged addresses and phone numbers.

Back at Mom's girlfriend's house, all they talked about were the two boys they met. I could feel the jealousy burning in my lungs and how it took my breath away. I knew I could never say anything, because seeing Susie so happy was another feeling that welled up in me.

Other than myself having a boyfriend, Susie's happiness was vital to me. In a way, I wanted to celebrate, but on the other hand, I just wanted to scream. We arrived home around eleven o'clock at night. We all went directly to Darlene and Virginia's bedrooms. I stayed with Darlene in her room, and Susie stayed with Virginia.

Late into the night, we could hear them both talking about the boys. We got up early and watched the sun come up. After breakfast, we all went to one of the rooms to listen to some records and talk for a while. It did not take long for the conversation to come around to the two boys.

Sitting there, I would again feel the pain of jealousy coming through. The sun has been up for a few hours. The heat and humidity increased by the second. There were very few clouds in the sky. It was a perfect, beautiful summer day. Darlene suggested that we all go swimming. Darlene and Virginia's parents had a new swimming pool built the week before we arrived, and it was not quite full yet, but it had enough water to go swimming. Mom had just bought Susie and me a new swimsuit.

For her being a conservative, these swimsuits were a little revealing. They had two pieces, with a small bra-like top and a pretty low-cut bottom, with strings of crisscrosses on each hip. In a way, I was a little embarrassed to be seen in it. I thought, well, I had nothing to lose, no one would see me in it anyway. We were in the water for a few minutes when Donald and Rodney pulled in along the curb.

As they exited the car, I tried to keep my body under water as much as possible. I still thought Rodney was so cute and was unsure what he would think seeing me in a bikini. I still had not accepted the way my body had developed. I wanted in the worst way for Rodney to see me as a young lady and not as an immature, undeveloped little girl, but I was unsure if this was the best way for him to do so. I still saw myself as that thin, homely girl from high school. I did not know at the time that my body had developed and my curves were showing off the young lady that I have become.

Having my confidence destroyed for so many years left me in doubt. I finally got out of the pool, but as soon as I did, I wrapped myself in a beach towel. Rodney, Donald, Susie, and Virginia sat at a table in the yard and talked for hours. Darlene and I walked to the house to get out of the heat. Still feeling a little down, I was afraid I would never see Rodney again. Mom and Dad came to pick us up later in the day. Susie told them about the boy she met. I went to bed not knowing what to expect next. What if Susie forgets about me? Now that she has someone else in her life.

I fell asleep and woke up in a slightly better mood. Still not knowing what the future holds for me, I tried my best to be happy for Susie. That afternoon, Donald called, and he and Susie talked on the phone for over an hour. Donald was also a shy boy and had never had a girlfriend before Susie. He asked if he could come to the house to see her, and she said, "Sure."

Later that afternoon, we watched as Donald's car pulled into the driveway. I was so surprised that when he drove up the driveway, I could see someone else in the car. Rodney was sitting on the passenger side. Why would he come to see Susie? This seems a little strange, but I was glad he was there. I figured, if he was here, he was not out with Virginia.

When I asked Donald why Rodney came with, he said, "I was unsure if I could find the house alone." So, I asked Donald why he was not out with Virginia, and he said, "Rodney does not like her that much."

I felt a little sorry for Virginia, but happy for myself. As Susie, sitting in the car for hours was not an ideal situation. Rodney would lie his head on the door to sleep. I would sneak out and peek in the window to look at him. Donald would come over three to four times a week. And with every trip, each visit, Rodney would be with him. I had left it slip one day and told Susie how cute I thought he was and that I liked him. She mentioned to Donald how I felt, and he told Rodney about my feelings.

One day, when they came over, Rodney got out of the car, walked over to me, and asked me if we could talk. I found out the reason he came with Donald was to meet me. From that day on, we were together as much as possible. He sat next to me, gently held my hand, and talked with a soft tone. Not knowing anything about him, he stole my heart. This was the second time I was in love.

The first time was not real and never would have been. I could tell this was real; it was so different. Mom and Dad could tell Susie and me were so happy with Donald and Rodney, so they allowed us to go with them. They had no reason to trust them, but they did.

There was a time when Donald's car was not running, and they had to take a city bus. Riding a bus meant they had to get on in Temple, go to Reading, get a transfer for a bus to Monton.

Getting off the bus in Monton now meant they had to hike a mile and a half up to the top of the mountain. Mom and Dad could tell that if Rodney and Donald were going to put in the effort and time to climb a mountain, they must be serious about their little girls. It worked both ways; if Susie and I wanted to go with them, we had to make that same trip down the mountain and back again.

Riding a bus to Temple took much longer than riding in a car, while driving a car would only take approximately twenty minutes, but the total trip by bus took around one and a half hours. I am not sure why Mom and Dad were not worried about us spending a whole weekend away from home. I believe they had trust in our ability to know right from wrong.

Rodney finally got his car. It was not much, but it was his. His dad had an old 1940 blue Oldsmobile parked in the backyard.

Rodney asked his dad, "May I have the old car?"

His dad replied, "Sure, "but it will need a little work."

It took him a few weeks to get it running, and one day he drove the car to pick me up. I was surprised to see him driving it. By this time, Donald's car was also running. Now both had their own car and could come to see us whenever they wanted. There were still a few more weeks before school would start. Rodney and Donald both had day jobs, but still managed to come to see us in the evening.

Every weekend, they took Susie and me somewhere, like a drive-in movie, a theater in Town, a ride in the country, or out to eat. Both of them were very good to us and treated us like queens. I can remember one day, Rodney picked me up at home and took me to downtown Reading. He parked the car on a lot behind the stores. We walk up the sidewalk to Pomeroy's Department Store.

Entering the store, there were two levels. The lower set of stairs led to the bargain basement. We went down to the lower level and walked down the center aisle.

The first item to catch my eye was a long blue winter jacket with white faux fur around the hem and each cuff. I could not believe it when he said that he wanted me to have it. They did not have my size, except for the one on the mannequin. He had them take the jacket off the mannequin so he could try it on. I was so proud and felt beautiful when putting it on. I knew that when school started, I would be the envy of even the popular girls. I was also going to be able to hold my head up high as I walked the halls, knowing that I had a boy's ring hanging around my neck. I will not need someone to try again, to take advantage of me, I was spoken for.

The year before our marriage, I spent most of my weekends at Rodney's Parents' house. Rodney's mom's name was Thelma, and his dad was Clarence.

Thelma was approximately 6 feet tall, while Clarence was only 5 feet 5 inches tall. Despite their differences, they had a good marriage. I was worried that our age difference would interfere with the relationship I was hoping to have with his parents. They put my mind at ease and treated me like their daughter. I slept in Rodney's bed, ate their food, and went on vacations with them. They made a few trips to the Pocono Mountains to go camping. I loved his parents as I did my own.

How could anyone guess these two boys would fall in love with Susie and me? Two girls from the country who were somewhat plain and not that smart. Two young men who are a few years older than Susie and I saw something in us that kept them staying with us for over 60 years.

My husband, Rodney. A Picture from Grade 9th or 10th

A Bodyguard

As Susie and I grew up, we never, for some reason, had a fear of physically being hurt by someone else. I am not sure if in the back of our minds, we always knew we had a bodyguard. Nelson, being a few years older than us, took the role of our protector. No matter what we were doing, he always seemed to be there. I never thought too much about his presents, but as I got older, I could look back and say, "Yes, he was there." His protection was an unseen part of our lives.

Nelson was an introvert, and in most cases, he would rather spend his days alone. He would never interfere in our lives, or even make his opinion known, but I could feel his affection. Now that I think about it, there were a few shy men in my life: Rodney, Donald, and now my brother.

When Susie and I were toddlers, Nelson would stay to himself more. It was not until Susie and I got older and the foster boys came into the house that I could see a change in him. I know he did not like the idea of Mom and Dad taking strange boys into our home. He was concerned for our well-being and our quality of life. His

Nelson's class picture, 1965

concerns were well-founded; no one knew how this would turn out. I thank God every day for a wonderful life.

While living at home, there were never any incidents of concern. Nelson spent most of his days in his room. He likes working on items, taking them apart, and rebuilding them. He had a great mind for scientific experiments.

Susie and I never felt any hard feelings towards any of the boys that came to live with us, but Nelson did resent the affection that Mom and Dad gave to kids who were not biologically born into our family. He let his feelings be known to me one day. He said that the affection and the things that Mom and Dad bought for the foster boys should have been his. I could see how jealous he was of the boys, by the way he did not interact with them. I know he tried to see why Mom and Dad needed more and more kids, but he never found what he was looking for.

Knowing that he loved Susie and me helped us deal with the situation. I wish we could have been closer, the way he felt, versus our feelings, left a barrier between us. We would never be close, as brother and sisters should be for the rest of our lives. This does not mean that I do not think about him. We could never agree on the lives we led; they were so different, but the love I still have for him cannot be denied.

As we turned the corner from childhood to adulthood, there

was still a way to go. To most people, we were no longer children, but still not adults. There were a few years in between that we did not know what we were. At times, I still wanted to stay a child, but in other circumstances, I wanted to be treated as an adult. I did not know about Susie, but my feelings were so conflicted at thirteen that I was unsure how to act. I still wanted the life of running in the woods and playing, but then I also wanted to be grown up and to be able to do the things that teenagers do. Seeing the world as a child and times as an adult was so confusing, I felt like I was back at Dorney Park, riding that roller coaster. My feelings were up one day and down the next. Mom could see how we were struggling with our feelings.

Now and then, she would take us aside and try to explain the facts of life to us, giving us some much-needed guidance. We appreciated her concerns and knew she was doing it out of love for us. She said that we would always be her little girls, but now it was time to create our paths in life.

She said, "Just act what comes normal to you at the time, either that of a child or an adult. Over time, the child will be left behind, and you will see what being a true adult is like."

I am so thankful to Mom and Dad for the love I received over the first thirteen years on this earth, and I know it will not stop there. I also want to thank Susie for being there for me at every turn of my life. To my older brother Nelson, even though we were never really that close over the years, I want you to know how much I do and always loved you.

Nelson, our older brother, had graduated from High School and was looking for a job. Susie and I were starting a new school year, being neither a Junior nor a sophomore. I was still not sure what path my life was to take.

Over the next year, my decision would be made clear. I felt that I had no other choice. I knew this was the only decision to give me the love and peace I have been searching for. If I stayed in school longer, I would learn nothing and only hate myself and everyone around me.

Senior High

Now that Susie and I were about to attend a new school and enter the tenth grade, we knew the bullying would be worse than the year before. The older the students grew, the more enjoyment they felt from being bullies. All I wanted was to go to school and come home with a sense of calm, but this never happened.

From the first day of entering the school, the bullies were lined up like a firing squad, just waiting for their chance to say something nasty. I knew entering the tenth grade would leave me with more hostility than ever before. I tried to go to my classes and not listen to the words and jesters that echo off of every movement I made.

Since Susie and I had been in different classes since the sixth grade, she did not know what had happened to me. One day, I wanted in the worst way to make friends and share my high school experience with someone. I was tired of being alone all day. Being treated as an adult was important to my ego. A few girls who were not in the popular group had become friends with Susie and me over the last few years. This friendship was okay, but it did not seem as close-knit as the other groups were.

Our bus arrived at the school a little earlier than normal. I had just opened my locker to get out my books and place some articles in it when one of the girls asked me if I wanted to go for a short walk around the school building. This sounded like a great way to interact and make new friends.

As we started out the doors and up to the side of the school, one of the girls pulled out a pack of cigarettes and asked me if I wanted one. I was not sure what to do at first since I had never smoked a cigarette before. I knew it was something I did not want to do, but on the other hand, I did want to fit in.

I was handed a cigarette, and one of the other girls lit it for me. I watched as they all took a few puffs on the ones they were holding. I guess it was my turn, so I did the same. After a few puffs, I started to cough. This seemed to amuse the other girls, and with a few puffs, I was no longer coughing. It was soon time for the school bell to ring, and school would start in a few minutes.

We all hurried to put out our cigarettes and hurried back to school. As I was sitting at my desk, the loudspeaker that was mounted on the wall came on. Someone on the other end announced that Sandra Henne was to report to the office. I could not imagine why I was sent for.

As I turned the corner to enter the office, I saw the same girls I had taken the early walk with. Someone reported us for smoking on school property. We did not know that we were doing anything wrong other than smoking. The pavement that went three-quarters around the school was considered school property.

We were all reprimanded and were given extra homework. You know what they say, "Live and Learn." Well, in this case, I did learn a good lesson. Just because someone else does something you know is wrong, does not mean you need to do the same just to fit in. If they were going to be my friends, I should have listened to my inner self and rejected the cigarette. If they rejected me for not smoking, then they were not my friends.

It was September of 1963, and school had only been in session for a few days. Would this be the year I feel safe in school? Or do I still have a bullseye on my back?

The only thing that helped me make my life in school bearable was knowing that Rodney would be coming over to see me later that night. I seem to go through the motions of being in school, watching the clock in every class. Every minute felt like an hour. I would doodle on my notebook cover, writing Rodney and Sandy hundreds of times.

My notebook was covered with our names. I would daydream about us being together for the rest of our lives and seeing what the world had to offer. I dreamt that we would have a perfect life like Ozzie and Harriet had on TV. I completed any homework, but this does not mean I understood what I read or wrote. I can understand how bullying in School can affect the rest of a person's life.

If Rodney had not come into my life, I could see my life going in a few different directions. Maybe, I would have climbed out of the bottomless pit I was in and ignored the worthless feelings that I was having.

Every day, the pain of getting out of bed, knowing what was waiting for me at school, was like being in hell, and coming home was Heaven.

Day after day, month after month, days were by so slowly. Halloween was in the past, and in a few weeks, it would be Thanksgiving. The temperature was changing from those warm summer days to bitter cold. There was an early snowfall that year. Mom and Dad invited Rodney and Donald to join the rest of the family for Thanksgiving dinner. This was the first large meal that we all spent together.

By the time they arrived for dinner, there was a dusting of an inch of snow on the ground. Knowing that Mom and Dad approved of them made me feel secure and loved by all of them. Having Mom and Dad consider my feelings, knowing what I go through every day at school, meant everything to me.

Everything was going along just fine for a while, until one day at School, when the world seemed to go crazy. I was sitting in my Social Studies class when over the loudspeaker, a voice announced that everyone was to report to the auditorium. Many rumors were circulating about why we were going there, but none could have been worse than what we were about to hear.

As soon as everyone sat down, listening to the loudspeaker, we heard a voice that sounded like a news broadcast. The day was Friday, November 22, 1963. Around 12:30, we heard a solemn voice start to speak. It was the voice of a male news reporter; he said that a few minutes ago, President John F. Kennedy was assassinated in Dallas, Texas.

Before the announcement, you could not hear yourself speak; the auditorium was full of everyone talking, and some even laughing. After the announcement, you could hear a pin drop. I could hear crying all around me. Even though we were only teenagers, we knew what this would mean for the world.

President Kennedy was a great leader and kept the world around us safe. He was loved by everyone, well, maybe not everyone, or he would not have been shot. The staff members, including the teachers, office workers, and most of the student body, were so upset with the news that they could not continue with the rest of the day.

Again, a voice came over the loudspeaker stating that school classes would be cancelled for the rest of the day. I hurried to my locker to gather my belongings and looked for Susie. We went outside to wait for our bus to pick us up and take us home. The sidewalk outside the school was full of students waiting for their buses, but the atmosphere was that of a family member passing away. I could not believe that even the popular students were quiet. There was no laughing or bullying, only the sound of students asking each other why, how, and who?

We were given no answers to any of these questions. As soon as we got home, Mom had the TV on. We went into the living room and sat on the floor, hoping to get answers to our many questions. Rodney and Donald called and asked if they could come over later. They had something they wanted to give us. After the awful day we had, anything would be an improvement. Mom made supper, and we all sat down to eat, but you could tell that things were not the same. Only the smaller kids who did not understand what had happened earlier that day were talking and laughing as normal.

After supper, Susie and I hurried to clear up the dishes before the boys arrived. I keep saying boys, they were no longer boys, Donald had just turned 19 in August, and Rodney had just turned 18 at the end of September. We were dating men at 14, isn't that a kicker?

Susie and I had no idea this would be the worst and the best days of our lives. We waited in our room playing records until they arrived. Mom yelled up the steps when she heard their car coming up the driveway.

They came into the house and we all sat at the kitchen table. We sat there for a while when Rodney pulled out of his pocket a small box.

He opened the box with a smile and asked, "Will you marry me?"

I looked down at the box, and there was a beautiful gold band with a tiny solitaire diamond ring. Donald also pulled a small box from his pocket and asked Susie the same question. Being only 14, it took a while for us to realize what had just happened.

As soon as I could speak again, I said "yes."

I heard Susie saying yes as if she was accepting a gift from God. To us, God had answered our prayers when we asked him to take us away from the bullies at school. Getting out of school was only a bonus; I did love Rodney with all my heart. I knew it would be another full year before we could even think of marriage, but if we were still together for the next year, I knew our marriage would work.

Going back to school on Monday will be a pleasure for a

change. How many popular girls can say they have a ring around their neck and a diamond engagement ring on their finger?

Unexpectedly, we no longer come across as homely as we were the week before. There still were those who did not believe we were engaged.

I proved this to them when Rodney parked his large blue Oldsmobile in front of the school and waited for me to come out. As I approached him, he was standing by the passenger's door. He leaned over and kissed me. I turned and looked over my shoulder. I could see a few of the popular girls and a few of the boys just watching us. He turned around and opened my door, and I got in.

As he drove away, I waved to the kids standing on the pavement with their mouths wide open. I know to some of them nothing would change the next day at school, but I least they could no longer call me a liar. Susie and I were now popular with the friends we already had. Christmas was only a few weeks away, and I looked forward to Christmas vacation. A few days away from the torment at school and more time to spend with Rodney.

I would spend more and more time at his parents' house. They were very kind to me and accepted me as one of the family. I would spend whole weekends at their home. Seeing how some other people live was an eye-opener.

Rodney's parents were a little old-fashioned. The house was small with tiny rooms. They had no hot water or bath facilities. To wash, they heated hot water in a kettle on the stove. They would pour the hot water into an enamel basin. They took the hot water, a wash cloth, soap, and a towel to their room to bathe. They had a kitchen sink and a toilet.

Rodney's bedroom was right outside the bathroom where the toilet was. There was no door, only a curtain that separated his room from the bathroom. It would be a year or so later that they had a water heater installed and a small shower.

When Rodney was a small boy, he had to walk over two miles each way to go to school. He learned as a young boy that if he wanted something, he had to work for it. Although his parents did not have much, they were very kind to those they liked. Rodney had two sisters, an older one named Shirley and a younger one named Vallane.

By the time I met Rodney, his older sister was married and had a few kids. Vallane did not take to me at first. She did not like a girl the same age as her, dating her brother. I could understand her feelings, after all, I was very young. She was afraid I would hurt him.

Christmas was here, and Rodney knew how much I wanted a pair of stretch pants. This was a new trend; these pants had stirrups on the bottom of each leg that went around the sole of the wearer's foot. Rodney took me shopping and bought me two pairs, a blue pair and a black pair. We still could not wear pants to school. I loved my pants, but I must admit that they were not too comfortable. After having them on for a while, they would hurt the bottom of my feet. I would have to take the stirrup off and let it rest on the back of my leg. He also bought me a beautiful mohair sweater. I do not remember what Susie got from Donald.

Celebrating the New Year, I remembered being at Donald's parents' house. Susie and I were enjoying the evening with some food we had made. The boys started drinking beer, which they were not used to doing. Since I met Rodney, this was the first time I saw him drinking. Neither one of them got ugly or abusive. They just got silly.

As the evening was getting closer to the midnight hour, both Rodney and Donald were drunk and started kissing the women on the TV Set. Rodney and I stayed at Donald's parents' house long enough to watch the ball drop in New York City on TV.

Rodney and I only had a short walk back the alley to his parents' house, so seeing him getting drunk was no big deal. Right after midnight, I walked Rodney back to the alley and helped him get into bed. He was a little sick for a while, so after throwing up a few times, he rolled over and fell asleep. Susie and I were turning fifteen in a few days, getting closer to the age where we could quit school and get married.

The rest of the year went on as usual. Still being bullied at school, I learned to deal with it. Rodney would come over almost every night. On the weekends, we would always plan to get away somewhere. Over a few months, we went to different places in the Poconos. We also went to Washington, DC, to see the cherry blossom trees, Valley Forge, Gettysburg Battlefields, Dorney Park, Hershey Park, many Movies, and just going for a ride. I was never bored when I was with him. You would think by this time, he would have tried to take advantage of me, but this did not happen until a few months before my sixteenth birthday. There was some petting going on, but no intercourse.

We had a few conversations about sex, but I was never pressured to lower my standards. I was only 15 and wanted to be sure I knew what I was doing and getting into. There could be consequences that neither one of us was ready for.

The summer of 1964 was a very warm one. One day, Rodney's sister Shirley asked Rodney and me if we wanted to go to Atlantic City with them the following weekend. Of course, I wanted to make sure it was alright with Mom and Dad, and see how they felt about me being so far away and spending the night in a motel room. Sure, it was not the first time I went far away from home, but I would always return home the same day.

Since we were engaged, Mom and Dad said it was ok, but I should call at least once to reassure them that I was all right. Shirley and her husband, Butch, came to Rodney's house early Friday morning, and we were on our way to Atlantic City. Arriving at the shore, I was so conflicted with myself. Since going all the way with Rodney made me nervous, I wanted tonight to be the night. Was I fooling myself? Was this the right time?

I would go back and forth in my mind for over two hours. I was planning on this being the night I went from a young girl to an inexperienced woman, but I was willing to learn. When packing for the trip, I made sure I took a bathing suit that I was not self-conscious wearing.

As we arrived and looked for a room, I asked Shirley how Rodney and I would get a room together.

She said, "Turn your engagement ring around and it will look like a gold wedding band."

I did as she said, and there were no questions from the desk clerk.

We spent the whole day on the beach, watching the sun move across the sky. Since the sun was so warm, the water was cold. The sun was bright and extremely hot, and no clouds were in sight. The beach was crowded, and the seagulls flew low, hoping to get some food.

Rodney and his sister spent hours roughhousing in the water a few feet off the shore. I entered the water only for a few minutes, knowing I would burn quickly. Rodney applied suntan lotion to my back and legs, but I still got a nice sunburn. Being so fair-skinned, I burned in a few minutes, not hours. Just the wind coming across the salt water, "with no sun," I would burn.

I love the beach, the water, and the sun, but they do not like me. Returning to our room, Rodney applied cooling lotion onto my back, legs, and arms. I was praying the sunburn would not ruin my plans for a romantic night. I looked like a red beet, but still got dressed to go out on the boardwalk. We met Shirley and Butch and walked up a side ramp towards the ocean. Strolling the full length of the boardwalk, we would stop now and then to play a game or two.

Rodney won me a stuffed animal. I carried it for the rest of our walk and would not let anyone else touch it. He won this for me. What a great man I have found to spend my life with. Seeing the love in his eyes as he handed me the stuffy confirmed my love for him. I knew this was the correct night to show him I love him with all my heart. We stopped at a few more stands to get something to eat. Before heading back to our room, Rodney bought me some ice cream. I was having a wonderful time and did not want it to end. I knew we would only have a few hours tomorrow before it was time to take that long ride home.

We went back to our rooms, and he watched me undress, but never made any move toward me. I did not try to hide from him, letting his eyes see me as a woman, not a little girl. His eyes watched every move I made. He was already lying on the bed as I approached him. He pulled the blanket aside and let me slide in next to him. As we lay close, I felt his hands moving up and down my body, and this time I did not stop him.

He got up on his arms, looking directly into my eyes, and said, "Are you sure you want to do this?"

I looked up at him and said, "It's time?"

Since neither of us has done this before, we took our time. I could tell he was nervous. I believe a good "How to Do" book would have helped. He held me close and was so gentle. After an hour, we lay quietly next to each other. Staring at the ceiling, I wonder if I was enough of a woman for him, and he was satisfied.

I closed my eyes and fell asleep in his arms. I felt so safe, so complete. Early in the morning, we made another trip to the boardwalk. We stopped for breakfast while waiting for his sister and her husband to join us. My sunburn made me uncomfortable, but I did not say anything. I was having such a great time, I did not want to do or say anything to ruin it.

We had to check out of our room by noon. As I packed our bags, I still did not know if we had traditionally made love. I knew from what I heard the first time would hurt a little, which it did, but was I reading something else into it, since I did have a bad sunburn? We both knew it would take a few more tries to be sure we did experience true love making.

We met up with Shirley and Butch and decided to walk the boardwalk one more time before leaving. We stood along the rail and watched the kids playing in the sand. Looking around, we observed all kinds of people entering the beach, fat, skinny, tall, short, and some very funny-looking ones. We watched as they struggled to walk in the sand, and lay down their beach towels as the wind blew them away. We watched for an hour or so, then it was time to head home.

I was saddened to leave Atlantic City; I wanted the last two days to last forever. Sitting in the back seat, on the ride home, he held me close. I hoped this was a sign that our lovemaking was everything he was wishing for.

This great getaway was bittersweet, knowing that returning to school was in my future. Summer was ending, and school would be in session in one week.

I was not looking forward to going back to school. Susie and I failed the tenth grade, but were told that since we only failed English, if we took tenth and eleventh grade English and, with all of our regular eleventh grade courses, and managed to pass them all, we would be promoted to the twelfth grade.

School started around the fifth of September, and we went to our classes as usual. Our wardrobe did not change that much from the year before, so the bullying has just picked up from where it had left off when school ended. Susie and I never asked for much, knowing that Mom and Dad had little money. Rodney did buy me a pair of Capezio shoes earlier in the Spring. I loved those shoes and wore them all summer and the start of the new school year. It got to the point that I wore the soles out, and there were big holes on the bottom. I would slide pieces of cardboard inside to cover the holes, having them last a bit longer.

It was around the middle of October; I was trying my best to get better grades because being a senior was in reach. One day in social studies class, the teacher gave us all a homework assignment. I was excited to do the research. Mom had bought a complete encyclopedia set of books. I waited after supper, and all the dishes were washed, to do my research.

I went to the living room bookshelf and looked for the book containing the information I was looking for. I found the story I knew would get me at least a B. I took the book to the kitchen table and copied the story word for word. I knew nothing about plagiarism and was so proud of my story. How could I go wrong with someone else's story?

The next morning, I gathered all my books, making sure I had my report. I did not have social studies until after lunch. I was feeling so confident and was looking forward to reading my report. A few students had read their reports, and it was my turn. I knew this was my chance to show that I did my homework, and it was to be the best thing I ever wrote. Getting up from my chair, I looked around the room, slowly walking to the front. The room was quiet, and I could hear my heart beating as I approached the teacher's desk. The teacher stood to the right of his desk, waiting for me to begin. I glanced over at him and turned to face the students.

As I started to read, I could see that the teacher had a strange look on his face. I was doing so well reading word by word, just like I had copied it from the book. I was not quite done reading when he asked me to stop. I looked over at him with a confused look on my face.

Why did he ask me to stop? Everything, in my opinion, was going great.

He walked over to where I stood and asked, "Where did you get this story? You know it is not true, and you made it all up."

In a split second, my heart stopped, and a moment of embarrassment consumed me. I could see an expression on every student's face, and it was not that of pity. He just gave them more ammunition to bully and tease me. I told him I got the story out of an encyclopedia that I had at home. He did not want any explanation and again said it never happened. Standing in front of approximately thirty students (classmates) and a teacher who had just called me a liar, I wanted to climb into a hole and pull it in behind me. I threw all my papers on the floor and ran out of the room. For me, this was the last straw.

Before entering the classroom, I managed to put the bullying behind me, but now a teacher is treating me as a criminal. I did nothing wrong. My self-esteem was destroyed. Giving the bully squad more ammunition was more than I could take. All I wanted was to get out of that school. After the bell rang, I entered the classroom to gather my belongings and walk out the front door. I did not go back to any more of my classes that day.

I went outside and cried until school was over and Susie came out. I told her what happened and told her that I was not going to do any more homework. I went back to school every day after that, but did nothing. Teachers like him are the reason a student gives up and quits school. I hoped to get a good grade on this report and feel good about myself, but now I will never be a senior. There was no use for me to try any longer.

Into my old age, the fear of speaking in front of a large gathering prevented me from exploring different avenues in my life. This teacher had destroyed my self-worth.

I managed to get through every day, and now it was mid-November. Susie and I came home from school and went to our room to change, when Susie told me that she missed her period.

I asked, "Do you think you are pregnant?"

She said, "I could be."

We sat on our beds for a few minutes, staring at each other. I looked at her and said, "I believe you'd better say something to Mom."

I do not know when she told Mom. Mom made a doctor appointment for her the following day. I was alone on the school bus ride home. I arrived home from school, and Susie was waiting for me.

I asked, "Well, are you pregnant?"

She said, "Yep."

She had already mentioned the possibility to Donald. She said he seemed happy about it and wanted to get married as soon as possible. We knew the marriage was out of the question until we turned sixteen. This would not be for another two months.

Our lives will change, and we are entering a new chapter in our lives. Marriage at the age of 16 is not going to be easy. Susie was to be a mother at a young age, and I will need to get a job to help pay the bills. We are jumping out of the pan and into the fire, a new life is facing us, and our future is what we make of it.

Our marriage may be amazing or a big mistake, but we have nothing to lose. Mom and Dad were worried and said that if marriage does not work out the way we hoped, we were welcome to move back home.

Susie and I in the year 1964